INNER
VOICE

INNER
VOICE

The voice of thought

MANUEL TRIGUERO

First edition: January 2022
Title: INNER VOICE
Cover image: Ralf
Copyright © 2022 Manuel Triguero
ISBN: 9798796414156

To my mother, of course.

Index

Introduction

Thoughts are nothing more than instruments of y-our own mind that show themselves there, for a certain time, and are exchanged for others in a constant movement that is never interrupted.

Sometimes this movement expands and gives rise to what we can call your inner chatter, your inner dialogue: that voice you hear in your head that is nothing more than all those thoughts that try to communicate with you, trying to lead you down a path that you end up walking.

The inner voice is what you often repeat to yourself when no one accompanies you. If you find yourself in a silent situation and observe everything you are thinking, you will realize that there is an accumulation of contents that are repeated with more assiduity.

In this new journey to our inner world, we will realize that there is a voice, an internal dialogue, which tries to communicate a series of thoughts that tend to be always the same.

And it is all because our attention is focused on those contents and not on others. For some reason, those thoughts are the ones that capture our interest the most, and that is why they are reiterated more frequently.

All these elements become part of an internal dialogue, of a voice that you constantly hear in your head and that is duplicated over and over again. It is like an automatic mechanism that we are born with, so it belongs to our very nature.

In reality, they are nothing more than judgments and reasonings that we make to ourselves, which are joined together in an internal discourse where we maintain a communication with ourselves.

You only become aware of this mental chatter when it is about a subject that is particularly interesting to you. Then you stop to observe what you are thinking about, sometimes you may even reflect on it. You try, in those cases, to look for new arguments to feed that conversation that sometimes you keep in your head.

In some moments, in that internal dialogue, you find support, as if it were another person talking to you and encouraging you, if you find yourself in a difficult situation.

Also your inner voice is what you say to yourself in certain cases, when you are trying to find an explanation to some subject that you are trying to understand at that moment.

In the same way, this inner chatter can also consist of questions that you usually ask yourself about something that is happening in a given situation.

In fact, everything that arises in your mind, at every moment, can become that voice, it can become part of that constant and repetitive internal dialogue.

It gains intensity when we are calm and we are not paying attention to anything in particular around us.

Then it acquires greater strength, it manifests itself through our internal dialogue, through thoughts that often accumulate disproportionately, usurping our energy.

In this inner speech, sometimes, there are incoherencies, deceptive reasoning, false beliefs that try to divert your attention and lead you to an unfounded confusion.

All this is emerging there, from that inner talk we have with ourselves, sometimes without a concrete objective.

This voice is absorbing thoughts trying to gather those that have a similarity and repeating them without rest, through an internal dialogue that we listen to and that we ourselves revive when we pay attention to it.

Therefore, we cannot deny the existence of this voice that never stops, which is like an internal conversation that we have with ourselves and that we somehow approve, without giving it the importance it deserves. We simply limit ourselves to follow the guidelines that it gives us through affirmations that we hear inside us, in the form of thoughts.

1. Inner voice

There is within us a world to discover, we only have to look inside ourselves to realize that there is a whole universe full of thoughts, images and emotions that are born from the deepest part of ourselves.

All these elements are in constant movement. If we stop to observe them we will learn their mechanism and the enormous influence they exert, without us often being aware of it.

All these aspects that we carry within us, seek to manifest themselves in some way. They use that inner voice that we all hear in our head repeatedly.

That voice is nothing more than an internal dialogue that we establish with ourselves where all those thoughts that arise in our mind flourish. It is nothing more than a faithful reflection of what we are thinking at any given moment.

When it uses thoughts that are too repetitive, it manages to capture our attention, in such a way that it marks the direction we should follow. Thus, in the end we end up performing a specific action related to that repetitive voice that shows us the way.

It is born unexpectedly, even if we are focused on something else, and as it is articulated we obey it, we become attached to it, as if we could not free ourselves from the force it exerts on us.

Sometimes a pause can be established, when we divert our attention towards something else that at that moment interests us, but when some time passes it returns again to extend itself again in our consciousness, thus wasting our mental energy.

When we least expect it, it expresses itself again, and so on. Its functioning and its reason for being depends on the interest and attention we pay to it.

It can appear when we least expect it, and also disappear if we divert our attention elsewhere.

Therefore, we could say that this voice evolves as time goes by. It rushes over us as if it were a current that changes its course depending on the circumstances.

In a way we could say that this voice is mechanical, because it acts without us being very conscious of it, in many occasions.

Sometimes, it can have a great energy, and at other times it can present itself as a weak voice, without any strength and without much influence.

This voice, on occasions, also makes us reflect, when it deposits in our consciousness an element that impresses us, in such a way that it quickly captures our attention and makes us try to look for explanations to reach a greater understanding of that matter.

CONTENTS

This voice can be centered on a determined subject and be for a prolonged time concentrated on that same subject. At other times, this voice can be composed of loose, punctual elements that are not related to each other. In the latter case, they are loose manifestations that are threaded together, even if they do not make much sense.

Sometimes their contents are transcendent and sometimes they are not. There are moments in which this voice diverts us towards subjects without much utility; and in other cases it can strive to lead us to a somewhat deeper dimension, using thoughts that are more related to ourselves, to our inner world and to all those things that are in the depths of our own being.

This voice does nothing else but claim those contents to turn them into a repetitive internal dialogue, which is reproduced in our mind without any kind of opposition on our part.

This voice is a constant association of ideas, thoughts, images that are distributed through our mind. It is like an extension where everything that we have in our memory, everything that we have collected through our experience, is exposed.

Somehow, what we think at a given moment is concentrated in that voice, which analyzes everything that happens, every decision we make. It is always alive.

If we were to stop to explore it, we would see with precision that it is composed of a whole set of mental representations that develop in our consciousness and that are linked to each other.

If we have the opportunity to analyze it, we will realize that they are nothing more than contents that we have stored in our memory and that arise at a given moment because we are under circumstances that make them significant for us at that moment.

In such a way that they begin to repeat themselves until they manage to capture our attention, until in the end they end up absorbing us and causing us to act according to that voice that sounds in our head.

Our inner voice is a signal that shows us the path to follow. It does not arise from a reflection, it simply exhibits itself in our mind spontaneously, without any moderation on our part.

They are thoughts

My inner voice is the voice of my own thoughts. Many times it takes over me and I can't help but pay attention to this constant chattering that goes on in my head.

My inner voice is made up of varied thoughts. Some may be very deep; others, however, are related to what I usually do in my daily life.

In reality, this inner voice is nothing more than the thoughts that constantly arise in my consciousness trying to group themselves together to find a common thread, a direction that allows them to continue flowing through my mind.

This voice is formed on the basis of impressions that arise from our memory. They are nothing more than thoughts that come together to form reasonings to which we attach importance, because they refer to subjects that are of some interest to us.

My inner voice is the narration that I continually make to myself through language. They are thoughts that rush and try to make themselves understandable in my mind. They spread through my consciousness trying to spread a series of ideas, of representations, that become part of my inner dialogue.

The inner voice contains all the thoughts, both the happy ones and those that cause us disappointment, since it is composed of all those contents that converge in our mind and that move from one side to the other.

They are elements that can accompany us for long periods of time, although they become weak and cease to be habitual if we do not pay attention to them and do not consider them, in such a way that they cease to affect us.

If we explore it a little, we will realize that it has more importance than it seems, because in it are grouped a series of thoughts that for some reason are relevant in those moments. So they are directing us in some way, trying to immerse us in a series of ideas and in a vision of things related to those specific thoughts.

DOES NOT STOP

Once it starts and settles in our mind, it tries to extend itself as long as possible, through expressions and comments that usually always go in the same direction, and that manifest themselves explicitly in our consciousness until they manage to conquer all our attention.

It has no limit, since it can be extended in time, depending on the circumstances. Most of the time it is understandable, even if it is plunging us even deeper into suffering of which we are often unaware.

It can remain there, without stopping, drawing conclusions about the world, life and those around us.

This voice can remain for prolonged intervals of time, since there is no moderation about it. It simply tries to expend energy, while it is enlightening us with a series of thoughts that we have previously fabricated in our mind, when we have tried to look for an explanation, a clarification to all those circumstances that we have had in front of us, when we have tried to understand them.

Sometimes we have the feeling that this voice never stops and we feel the need to free ourselves from it. We stubbornly repeat constantly a series of ideas in our head, to the point of insanity, because we fall into the deception of this mechanism that traps us, that imprisons us and makes us join some thoughts with others, so that this process is constantly repeated and has no end.

This is why this voice envelops us and we become attached to it, in such a way that it does not diminish with time; on the contrary, it grows, it grows more and more, through all that multitude of thoughts that are chained one to another and that break our internal balance, since they prevent that internal calm that we need to stop thinking, to move away from all that mental noise that weakens us, from flourishing.

It is difficult to stop it. It does not make any distinction as to the kind of thoughts it collects, it does not have a special inclination for a specific kind of thoughts: it simply uses those that are most repeated in our mind, according to the mental structure that we have created for ourselves by strengthening a certain kind of contents.

It is a mechanism that we cannot get rid of so easily, since it is very resistant to change and we cannot expel all those thoughts without effort, since they are scattered all over our mind in a dispersed way, in a disorder that we cannot control. From there they germinate, as they manifest in our consciousness.

Those that are more significant, stand out over others with less importance; the latter are erased, if we do not pay due attention to them.

If we limit ourselves to follow it, this voice expands and has no limits; it is like an internal noise that breaks the silence and ends up capturing our attention through all those thoughts that are reproduced in it.

2. How it influences us

Everything we think has a consequence, whether we put it into practice or not. Everything that rushes through our mind and settles in that internal communication we have with ourselves has a consequence.

If I don't pay attention, my inner voice can lead me to emptiness, it can separate me from who I really am. It can also determine the direction in which I have to walk, because they are thoughts that extend throughout my consciousness, that have their own autonomy and can lead me down uncertain paths.

If I am not conscious and I have the habit of letting myself be carried away by its impulse, my inner voice can deteriorate the way I observe reality, since it can flood me with many prejudices and create a disorder in my own reason, in the way I understand the world around me.

If I allow my inner voice to become strong, it can make my life a desert, divert me from my true purpose and make me live in permanent agitation, through irrational thoughts that move freely through my mind.

If I allow myself to be dominated by it, I will not conduct myself correctly. My decisions will not be the right ones, because there will be no coherence with what I really am, with what I really intend to do.

If I let myself be conquered by my own thoughts, by my mind and by all those meaningless representations, I will not know how to face adversity, because I will have an inaccurate vision of the world around me, which will take possession of me and will hide the truth from me, which only shows itself when there is clarity in the mind, when things are observed from another dimension, freed from the deceptions of thought.

If I accept everything that my inner voice dictates to me, I will always be in the same place, I will not advance, because it always runs in the same way: associating the same contents, invading me with the same thoughts and always trying to lead me in the same direction, along a path that has nothing to do with what really matters, with what I really am.

UNCONSCIOUSNESS

If you remain unconscious for long periods of time, your thoughts will be invariable, they will absorb you in such a way that your way of thinking will always go in the same direction, because of the abundance of the same contents.

The unconscious movement of the mind always works in the same way: it is based on a series of repetitive elements that little by little occupy all the space of your consciousness, in such a way that they leave an imprint that influences your reasoning and even your own judgments, about everything that happens to you at any given moment.

Your unconsciousness spreads throughout your mind, in a clear way, if you do not put a distance and move away from the movement of all those thoughts that crowd in that space and that little by little are tied, establishing chains of similar contents that are associated, until they manage to determine what you should do and what you have to think at a certain moment.

In the end, all this becomes an inner voice that tries to guide you, to lead you along a specific path towards an uncertain territory. This voice, composed by your own thoughts, penetrates you and in the end it is so insistent that you end up obeying it blindly.

In those moments you are not aware of the consequences of following that voice in your head, you do not care if it can lead you to frustration or situations that can cause you suffering, you just abandon yourself to it trying to persevere in the direction that it marks you.

All this can cause you to wander aimlessly for a long time, to remain in confusion and to spend too much energy on things that are not worthwhile, that do not materialize in something that is useful to you.

WE GOVERN

You cannot become obsessed with what is constantly going on in your head, for if you do, you will end up being determined by your own thoughts and they will rule over you.

Everything begins with a thought that arises in our inner voice. At that moment our calmness is altered and an idea begins to expand in our mind, with the idea of determining us, in such a way that it marks the path where we must orient ourselves.

Generally we follow it - we are always inclined to

follow what we think at any given moment - even if it is inexplicable or has serious consequences for us.

We opt for the simplest path, so we allow ourselves to be influenced at every moment by that inner voice that is growing inside, as we pay attention to it and give it importance.

We accept everything that comes from that voice, from that inner dialogue that drives us forward, even if some approaches are confusing and irrational.

In reality, we do not intervene much either. We simply limit ourselves to obey, even if all those thoughts are altering us inside, creating an instability or, what is even worse, a suffering that is affirmed with the passage of time, causing an anguish that little by little integrates itself in our whole body.

It is like a magnetic force that little by little overcomes us, in such a way that in the end it dominates us, trapping our attention, making us limit ourselves to repeat over and over again a series of contents that grow in our consciousness. We will perceive that it is like a flow, like a current that repeats itself if we do nothing to avoid it.

Through this inner voice that we all have, all those impressions that we have in our mind are precipitated in a mechanical way and that somehow dominate us, as they are exposed one after another.

In this way, this voice, treasures a great power, because it multiplies a great quantity of mental contents without us exercising any type of moderation, in such a way that it makes them spread through our conscience and that they do not disappear.

Then, with time, it becomes difficult to remove and displace all these contents to another place. Once they remain there, they influence our character, our own personality, because we allow ourselves to be infected by them.

In this way it grows within us, it determines what we should think, our decisions and what we should focus our attention on. Somehow it is a voice that governs us imperceptibly, occupying practically all our mental activity. We follow it immutably, even if it leads us to a fateful destination.

We have to be aware that it is something we have to live with. Therefore, we must raise our attention a little more to realize that we should not allow ourselves to be dominated by it.

Our thoughts are amplified in such a way that they manage to take control of us, of our attention, so that we forget everything else and we only focus on those thoughts that trap our will and from which we cannot detach ourselves, since they are elements that are constantly repeated, that insist on a series of ideas that are strengthened as we pay attention to them.

The thoughts that acquire a certain power, begin to reproduce themselves more frequently, and in the end they are the ones that end up dominating us, the ones that manage to determine us.

When we give them importance, they acquire a greater thrust, because they make our decisions depend on what is showing in our conscience at that moment. As there is usually no moderation on our part, in the end we allow ourselves to be influenced by all those impressions coming from that voice.

All those thoughts, all those ideas that form our inner voice, determine us, as they are impregnated in us. They are inserted in our consciousness, until at the end they occupy all the space.

They influence our way of discerning, our way of reasoning and they control even our own actions and the information that passes through our mind, in such a way that they also penetrate even our own reflections.

It gives us direction

If we pay attention to our inner voice, we will perceive that many mental contents, which are also manifested in that permanent internal dialogue we have with ourselves, somehow limit us, marking the path we should follow, the thoughts we should pay attention to.

If we do not manage to be conscious, our decisions will be determined by this kind of thoughts that are stored in our mind unconsciously, contaminating our way of seeing the world, our way of interpreting reality. If we do not remedy them in time, they will influence the direction we take at any given moment.

This inner voice that we all have influences us in some way, makes us decline our steps towards a certain direction, abandoning other paths.

In some way it is delimiting us, pointing out the path we have to follow. We simply accept it without further ado. We are not the ones who actually decide, but rather we allow ourselves to be dominated by this voice that little by little is articulated through all those thoughts that circulate through our consciousness, without any kind of opposition on our part.

We rush to execute what it dictates to us, even if some things are unpleasant, or are not of our interest.

That is why, if we follow it, sometimes it can lead us to disorder, to abandon our true path and to distract us in a series of tasks that in reality do not have a concrete purpose, or are not beneficial.

Everything we think is transferred to our judgments, to that voice that we all have that murmurs each of the thoughts that arise in our mind.

All these contents are transformed into ideas, beliefs that propose a way to solve the difficulties we face every day.

All that chant of thoughts occupies a space inside our conscience; they guide us in some way; they mark the direction we have to follow and the decisions we have to take before each one of the facts we face.

That is why we must consider that all this that we have in our mind, which becomes visible through an inner voice that constantly repeats itself, has a great influence on us; on what we do and on the way we are in the world.

IT MAKES US ACT MECHANICALLY

This inner voice, composed of automatic thoughts, can make you act in a mechanical way, without giving you time to reflect and take time to find the meaning of what you are doing; it only tells you what you should do, without telling you if it is good for you or not.

If we allow ourselves to be conquered by this voice, we will act in an automatic and unconscious way. Many of our actions will not be guided by logic, they will not be understandable.

We will not find explanations for many of our behaviors, which we will limit ourselves to repeat while obeying the orders of this voice that determines us internally, while we forget about ourselves.

It is like a force that takes over your will, that in those moments you do not know how to moderate, and that converts all your thoughts into specific actions that in the end you try to repeat, even if some of them do not have a concrete purpose, a determined end.

If we live in laziness and allow the mind to take over us, it will establish in our lives a mechanical way of acting that will keep us active, performing repetitive actions that deep down we consent and approve, but that will have nothing to do with who we really are, because they take over our will and come to have control over what we do or what we think at a given time.

IT HELPS US TO ESCAPE

We are always trying to escape, without giving importance to what really matters. We insist on concentrating on issues that often transport us to another strange reality. In the end, we end up elaborating a world to our own measure, often false.

We often lose our balance, especially when we let ourselves be overcome by discouragement and allow anguish to take hold inside. Then we are flooded by a whole set of thoughts whose only purpose is to rob us of our calm.

All this appears in our inner voice, which is where what we think at any given moment emanates. All this is impregnated in our inner voice, which slowly moves us to another area, through the use of the language of the mind that are the thoughts.

These contents become stronger as they envelop us from the inside. If we feel an affinity with what we are thinking at any given moment, we will immediately feel identified with those contents and they will begin to reproduce themselves in greater quantity, up to an indeterminate number.

Sometimes we use this inner voice to escape, when all those fantasies that are only the product of our imagination are manifested in it. They cause a whole imaginary world to spread over us, through a series of expressions that expand in our consciousness.

We must be attentive to all these signs, because they create a fence inside our own mind that little by little consumes us, in such a way that in the end it makes us live in a world created through our own imagination.

CAN LEAD US TO SUFFERING

My inner voice spreads throughout my mind, little by little. It tries to expand when my attention is focused on some representation that catches my attention.

Then my thoughts increase and begin to lengthen in time. If those thoughts are negative, my inner voice will begin to torment me; it will not consider the consequences for me of that disturbing pressure when thorny elements begin to join in, causing anguish and sadness to grow.

This inner voice is the beginning of everything. It can visibly lead you into a heap of complications, without any foundation. It can be the nourishment of your own sadness, without you even realizing it.

Our inner voice can affect us if we let it. It can trap our attention and accumulate a set of emotions that we cannot escape from, once they settle in our mind.

It can sow restlessness and keep us from serenity, if this voice is accompanied by a combination of negative thoughts. If they remain in time and move away, we can come to accept them over time, in such a way that they can shape our personality.

If we allow ourselves to be flooded by all these contents, we will live in a permanent agitation, which will increase if we allow all these representations in our mind.

We do not stop to clarify if what we are thinking at those moments is beneficial or not. In many cases we do not reflect on what is in our mind, we simply let ourselves be carried away by the spell of that internal voice that slowly fills us with contradictions that in some way affect us, because they envelop us in a discomfort that in the end causes us suffering.

Sometimes it can be harmful, especially when it comes loaded with toxic thoughts that we have also accumulated in our memory from our past experiences. When this kind of content crowds our consciousness, it can steal our inner calm, so much so that it can cause agitation that can last for a long time. On these occasions we experience negativity and suffering that take hold of us.

We only need to look at our internal discourse, at all those thoughts we have daily about the world and about ourselves. In it we will find all those contents that try to alter us in some way.

All those thoughts that develop in our mind, are then extended in that inner voice, in that inner dialogue. It is there where all those elements that first arise in our mind and that sometimes submerge us in a wrong world where restlessness and anguish reign.

Confusion

Sometimes, this voice harasses us in such a way that it penetrates into the deepest part of ourselves, in such a way that sometimes it immobilizes us. If we live pending of this voice, we can feel a permanent bewilderment.

Faced with this wealth of contents, it is easy that in many occasions we fall into confusion, since they are elements that appear in a disorderly way.

In most cases they are thoughts on which we have not had the opportunity to reflect. Many of them become irrational, they do not follow a concrete logic. In such a way that they make us separate ourselves from reality very easily, and that we fall into a daze through all that confusion that spreads through our mind and from which we cannot free ourselves.

Everything that torments us can also be included in that inner voice, which uses all the contents that are represented in our mind and manages them according to the attention we pay to them.

In many occasions it can become incoherent and disordered. It can use contradictory thoughts, many of which can even be irrational.

If we have the opportunity to observe it, we will realize that it can sow doubt, especially when thoughts that do not help us to understand the reality we are living are associated with it.

In these cases it becomes an inner dialogue that is

always stuck in the same place, without clarifying anything about the reality of the world we are living in.

If we do not diminish this voice, it is easy for confusion to take hold of us, for restlessness to rise in our inner world. All the thoughts that manifest in our mind have an effect that can go deep inside.

If we let ourselves be abandoned and follow our inner voice, our judgments may not be guided by true understanding and confusion may take over.

In some cases this voice can sow confusion, if we are dealing with disordered thoughts that are far from reason, from logic.

This voice can become irrational, so that it can lead us astray, derail us from the right path, lead us away from the truth and make us interpret reality in a faulty way.

In this way it will create illusory representations of the world that will be nothing more than inaccurate inventions that will develop in our own mind and spread further if we pay attention to them.

In this way our inner voice will create a confusion that will lead us to unhappiness and discouragement. If we do not remedy it, it will slowly destroy us, as we abandon ourselves to it, in such a way that in the end we will feel helpless, when the murmur of that inner dialogue takes over all our reasoning, our judgments, all the representations that circulate in our mind.

If we allow that inner chatter to contaminate us, confusion will spread, while a great number of unproductive negative thoughts will keep us away from our true purpose. We will be submerged in a world without exit, where we will remain for a prolonged period of time.

Conflict

This voice always accompanies us, and sometimes it makes us lose our balance when it exposes information that we find difficult to understand. In these cases it becomes necessary for us to reflect on that kind of content related to a series of ideas that transport us to a wrong interpretation of reality.

They are thoughts of which, sometimes, we are not sure, that appear there in a disorderly way and that in principle we do not reject; we allow them to join one with the other and that they separate us little by little from reality, from the truth of things.

When we do not understand very well all these contents, we feel inside a restlessness that little by little eliminates our tranquility.

When there are things that we do not understand or to which we do not know how to look for a precise solution, a feeling of uneasiness, of conflict is transmitted within us. We perceive that there is an alteration that breaks our internal balance.

When our mind is full of obstacles, all these concur in that inner voice, in that inner dialogue that we all have. Then we feel an internal disturbance that spreads to our innermost depths.

If we allow ourselves to be exalted by that voice, we will lose our inner balance, which is what makes us always walk on the path that we must not abandon: the path that leads to our true purpose, outside the imaginary deception of our own thoughts.

If we feed this internal discourse, which is often produced in our mind, we strengthen it without realizing it.

We must be aware that it is the origin where our reasoning is established. If in it we strengthen the conflict and all that negative current of toxic thoughts, which many times circulates in our mind, we will find ourselves with a negative internal chatter that will slowly mortify us, disturbing our calm and creating a suffering that will spread.

ENGAGEMENT

Sometimes, this inner voice can be a lie that spreads through our consciousness and gradually disorients us, making our judgments incorrect.

In such cases we can be under the deception of our own mind, where sometimes a series of thoughts are concentrated far from the truth, from the authentic reality.

When I abandon myself to my inner voice, it overflows me, because it makes me organize a series of contents that steal my calm and that in many occasions lead me to deception, to things that are not achievable, that are not possible.

I give them importance, because they are constant thoughts that little by little absorb me in an extraordinary way, while I let myself be abandoned in a naive way and they take possession of me and prevent me from contemplating other alternatives, from listening to other kinds of different thoughts.

It can break your tranquility in a given moment, if you let yourself be carried away by the excitement of its messages: of all those thoughts that throb in your mind constantly and that little by little are overflowing you without stopping, without hardly having a break to find clarity, to regulate all that frenetic activity that does not stop and that is marking your path through an invisible inner speech, which sometimes invents a false reality.

If we devote time to this voice and let ourselves be impressed by it, we will never find order in our mind. We will not be able to reflect coherently on the reality we see, both outside and inside ourselves. We will let ourselves be amazed by all those contents and images that are repeated over and over again.

If we let ourselves be carried away by all those messages that we establish in that internal communication that we have, we will fall into the deception of the mind. We will never come to appreciate the truth of things, nor what is beyond our own thoughts. Our life will always be a life full of constant obstacles and we will never find that inner harmony that only arises when that inner peace grows within us that changes everything, that eliminates all that inner turmoil that we often suffer when disorder spreads.

If we allow ourselves to be transported by all those thoughts that are born in our mind, our light will be extinguished. We will not be ourselves, since we will limit ourselves to imitate everything that is reproduced in our consciousness, even if it is a fallacy, a deception or has nothing to do with what we really are.

We simply allow ourselves to be deceived by that inner speech, by that chatter, in such a way that we end up separating ourselves from what we really are, from what we should do to be coherent. We let that voice be the one that guides us, the one that controls us.

If you have any concern, it is fostered by your inner

voice, which is used to repeat and to always turn over the same issues, even if they cause you a strong extortion or a great break inside.

That which is agitated in your inner world, is presented in the form of thoughts, through that dialogue that is your inner voice, which never stops, which is always in progress trying to give continuity to a series of ideas that are constantly repeated.

Sometimes we fall into the trap of letting ourselves be fooled by all those inconsistent thoughts that we repeat to ourselves, so that we allow ourselves to be altered by them, allowing them to change our mood.

Only by being aware will we gain greater security, because we will not let ourselves be carried away by the deception of the mind. We will find out where is the beginning of all things, of what irritates us, of what confuses us, of what disorients us.

If we manage all that information that is generated within, in our consciousness, we will evolve properly, we will move through the world and the right direction and we will make use of our best capabilities, because everything we do will be in line with what we are, with what we really want to do in every moment, in every situation.

We will not let ourselves be dominated by the deception of the mind, which often rushes upon us, filling our consciousness with contradictions, convulsions and fatalities that lead us to darkness, to live in the mist.

Unreal elements

Sometimes a concentration of thoughts spreads that

prevent us from reasoning. In these cases there is a madness inside that dominates us. A series of impressions accumulate, producing similar ideas during certain periods of time.

In those moments we would like to disconnect, but it is not so simple. We are enveloped, enclosed, in a swarm of thoughts that flourish without rest and to which we become accustomed, while they erode us from within.

Sometimes we feel that we are being burned, through an extensive movement of images that create an illusion: the deception of the mind. They have the ability to spread, in our own consciousness, a false reality that separates us from the world.

All this hustle and bustle of unreal elements, then emerges in our inner voice. That is why it often seems so far from reason, because it is composed of deceptive thoughts that evade us, that take us away from the truth, that reproduce a parallel world full of conflicts and battles that create a suffering that subdues us little by little.

Do not let us be surprised

You have an enormous power in your hands. If you do not take it into account or do not know it, you will never be able to free yourself from the deception of your own mind, you will not be able to stop all that suffering that repeats itself and that constantly upsets you.

It only consists of not allowing yourself to be surprised by all that gigantic movement of thoughts that run through our consciousness and that try to propagate themselves with a determined purpose. It is there where everything we end up doing throughout the day resides. Everything that starts there eventually ends up in a certain action or behavior.

If nothing changes inside, everything we manifest outwardly will not change either.

It is a matter of separating ourselves, in some way, from all that internal murmur of thoughts and ideas that try to lead us in a certain direction.

In this way we will be able to put some order in our lives, reestablish mental balance and diminish all that confusion that entangles us and that is acquired when there is no clarity in what we think.

3. How to moderate it

This voice agitates us, because it moves freely throughout our consciousness without a concrete order, without moderation on our part.

It is therefore necessary that we tame, in some way, this inner voice that we all carry inside, especially when it tries to give us a series of negative messages about ourselves and about the world in which we live.

If we want to live in peace and have order within, we must disregard this voice that tries to captivate us with thoughts that, being so repetitive, end up overflowing us, suppressing our inner calm and that tranquility that we should always maintain.

On these occasions we need to moderate this voice, to leave aside all those signals that are like a whirlwind that takes over our own imagination, filling our conscience with irrational beliefs.

It is we who must moderate, in some way, that which is within our own conscience. If we allow ourselves to be dragged by every impression that arises in our mind, by all those thoughts that our inner voice produces, we will not find clarity, order; we will live in a permanent conflict that will entangle us without stopping.

If we stop this internal dialogue that we have on many occasions, we will manage to somehow clean our mind of all that noise that is frequently agitated through all those thoughts that absorb us little by little, without us intervening too much, because we only participate in a passive way favoring all those contents, many of which are not profitable and do not lead to any benefit.

If we manage to diminish it, we will be able to establish a certain order within all that confusion of thoughts that increase in our conscience and that become stronger with the passage of time.

We have the obligation to orient all those thoughts, no matter how small they may be. Depending on the capacity of control that we have over them, so will be the control of ourselves.

We only need to establish a certain moderation on all that mental activity that in the end ends up becoming an unconscious programming that is transformed into a series of concrete habits.

If we look inside, in that space of our own mind where all those thoughts that we constantly have move and shift, we can intervene, in some way, directing our judgments and clarifying our reason.

All this will help us to cultivate common sense, objectivity and the search for truth. We will move away, in this way, from all those wrong beliefs and fantasies that create an imaginary world for us.

CONTROL

Sometimes thoughts pile up in our mind; this is when the inner voice becomes stronger. In these cases we cannot separate ourselves from it, although it tries to deceive us by mixing some things with others without any sense.

If we do not know how to stop it, sometimes we may have the feeling that we are going crazy. That is why it is necessary to control it in some way, especially when it is a little hostile. It is the only way to reduce all that inner noise that in many occasions spreads inside agitating us.

We do not know many processes behind this voice that we all have, but with a little willpower we can prevent it from increasing; we can try to isolate it in some way.

This mechanism, although it is imposed on us, we can moderate it, we can reach a certain control over it. For this it is necessary to reach a deep knowledge about the functioning of all these processes that lead us to the constant repetition of the same thoughts during a certain time.

CHANGING THE DIRECTION

Somehow we remain submissive to that inner voice that tries to subordinate us through a series of contents that it stores in our conscience, within that internal dialogue that we maintain and that rushes along our mind, without a determined direction.

If we concentrate on it, we can somehow change the direction or simply disregard it, fix our gaze on another matter, establishing a distance from what we are thinking at that moment; it is the only way to free ourselves from this bondage, if we change our attention to another place where there is less confusion; it is the only way to escape from many irrational ideas that we are constantly repeating.

In this way, this inner voice does not become gigantic; in this way its representations fade away, trying to find a way out of our own mind, which is where all the conflicts start, where all those confusions that surround us are raised without us being able to clarify them.

If we get used to observe all that is composed in our conscience, we will understand our way of thinking: why we constantly feed a series of ideas that end up determining us, convincing us.

If we investigate all these impressions, we will observe how they move, how they evolve within our consciousness. We will discover that the only way to diminish them is to renounce them, to incline our attention towards another place. Then they will stop happening one after another, and that inner communication we have with ourselves will decline.

We can establish a new direction in our way of thinking. We only have to pay attention to all those contents that go around in our mind without interruption. They are nothing more than expressions of our memory that have been founded over the years and that are the product of the information we have been acquiring through experience, through all those events that have happened to us over time.

Only in these cases, all our alterations will disappear. We will be able to recover our peace of mind and our spirits, we will stop feeling dominated by all those thoughts that try to annul us, when they rush through our mind.

Only if we are conscious we will understand how

these kinds of representations are created, how they are fixed in our mind composing structures of thoughts that rise more and more as we pay attention to them; in such a way that in the end they end up limiting us, marking the path we have to take, the direction we have to follow.

If you observe all this, this voice stops losing intensity, stops guiding you, stops governing you, stops directing all those thoughts.

YOU CAN LEARN FROM IT

If you want, you can learn from your own inner voice. Everything that is expressed in it is based on all those thoughts that arise in your mind, often unconsciously. As they are very abundant, they are directing you and transferring you to another reality, without you being very conscious of it.

If you observe carefully, you can realize how that voice can divert you, make you think about other things or erase from your consciousness what really matters. You can see the greatness of this automatic mechanism that is of great importance to your own well-being.

If you carefully analyze its messages, you will realize that they are very repetitive, so that in many occasions they remain the same for a long time.

As the days go by, you feel that you cannot get rid of them and that somehow you adapt to them without giving them too much importance; your way of acting becomes accustomed to these contents.

In a way, this inner voice is shaping you from the inside; changing your way of being and thinking. For you, this fact is insignificant. You just limit yourself to follow its indications, while a whole structure of thoughts is created within you, which accumulate and occupy all the space of your consciousness, without any moderation on your part.

If these contents are not beneficial and do not have an order, they can destroy you little by little, while you follow the current of these thoughts.

It is only when you feel that there is some kind of disturbance within you, because of all these elements that are constantly arising, that you feel a certain interest in the origin of all that is happening. In such a way that you come to find the cause of all those useless contents that have been asserting themselves in your mind, without your consent, breaking your calm, occupying all the space of your consciousness.

In those moments you understand with clarity that you can choose, that you can establish an order in all those elements that are feeding your brain, that are maintaining that structure that sustains what you are and what you do.

In those moments you can take a breath and observe with clarity what it is that is trying to force you, that is coercing you. You can clarify many things and correct many negative thoughts that insist on dominating you and manifestly creating a series of problems within you that in the end lead you to a suffering that little by little is confusing you, that is dazing you while you remain distracted with other things, performing other tasks.

4. Be aware

The best way to moderate our inner voice is to be aware that this happens inside us, that there is a mechanism that orders us what we have to do, without us being very conscious of it.

We simply have to be aware of all those thoughts that are agglomerated in our mind, which are the basis of that inner voice that is providing us with a constant chattering in many situations, especially in those in which we are alone.

If we manage to distinguish properly when it is produced, when it tries to seize us, we can manage to numb it. In this way we clean a little our mind eliminating all those repetitive contents that little by little are absorbing us, obtaining that slowly we go away molding to them.

If we listen to it attentively, we will realize that, in reality, it is a mechanical process that tries to consume energy that at that moment we are not spending on other things.

If we are aware of this, it is easier for us to be conscious of this movement that is created in our consciousness, that remains for a long time and that is sending us messages without rest.

We have to cut that movement by being aware of how it works, understanding in detail why that voice repeats itself with the same thoughts trying to govern us, to reach the mastery of our own mind.

Once we become aware of this, once we discover that this exists within us, we will pacify that inner voice and bring clarity. So that all those confusing thoughts will diminish and in this way the mental darkness that many times we have incorporated into our mind without realizing it will disappear.

It is important to be aware that, on many occasions, that voice -which comes from within ourselves- is not subject to the truth; it may be distanced from reality itself. That is why we should not allow ourselves to be confused by it. We must try to silence it when it tries to limit us.

Once we are aware of it, it will slowly dissolve; it is the best method to re-establish order within us, to give continuity to that calm that must always reign in our inner world.

In this way, that inner voice will gradually become hidden, it will cease to be uncomfortable and disconcerting. We can diminish it, make it smaller, if we are aware that this is happening within ourselves.

It is a way of releasing suffering. If we allow it to spread, it will remain inside for a long time, so we must expel it at the slightest opportunity we have.

To do this, it is necessary to be aware and attentive to all that is produced in our consciousness, which then translates into that voice, in those repetitive thoughts that are slowly hitting us and that are marking our own actions.

If we are not aware that this process exists within

us, all these elements follow one after the other and impose on us a certain way of thinking, which we end up accepting without further ado.

LOOKING FOR A SPACE

In general, throughout the day, we direct ourselves in an unconscious way, letting our own mind be the one that marks the direction we should follow.

There are other moments, however, when we have a certain degree of awareness on our part. In these specific cases we realize what we are thinking at that particular moment, and we can decide for ourselves without being carried away by that automatic stream of thoughts that takes control very easily of our actions and behaviors and what we should think at every moment.

These specific occasions, in which we are conscious, are rare. They arise naturally, in some people more than in others. However, what is important is that these situations are sought after, that they are moments in which there is an intention on our part to reduce all the influence that our mind exerts on us.

It is about looking for those spaces, throughout the day, in which we try to be a little more conscious than we usually are. We just need to pause briefly, from time to time, to realize and be aware of what we are doing at that moment; where we are; what thoughts are circulating in our mind.

With this we will gain a higher level of awareness that will be beneficial, since with this we will be able to stop behaving like a robot; we will put aside our automatic behaviors and regain control of ourselves.

It is a good exercise that will help us to situate ourselves; to see where we are in each moment and why we do the things we do. In a way it will also help us to control our own habits, in case they are not healthy.

PAYING ATTENTION

Sometimes I stop to observe my inner dialogue: all those thoughts that are reproduced automatically and without rest inside my own mind.

I believe that it is extremely important to pay attention to this inner chatter, because it is the cause of our own suffering.

We must pay attention to all that is propagated in our mind, to all those representations that spread through our consciousness trying to enlarge themselves.

If we pay attention we will find the way to manage all that mental activity that tries to drive us. We will observe the agitation that exists within, through all those impressions that occupy our consciousness, coming from our memory. We will realize that, in them, in each thought, is where the suffering is generated and all those internal affections that we suffer, and all our worries and the anguish that slowly weakens us.

We only have to pay attention to that voice, to know that it exists and that it can trap us at any moment, under any circumstance, through a series of concrete thoughts that repeat themselves over and over again in our mind, without us being very conscious of them.

If we pay attention to our inner voice, to that inner chatter that we all have, we can clearly see that all those contents manifest themselves there. We can carefully observe that which creates difficulties, inconveniences, as well as all those representations that are constantly repeated and that try to join with other similar ones to try to create a certain vision of the world; sometimes very far from reality itself.

All this information will not be extinguished so easily, because it has always remained there. In some concrete situations it emerges into our consciousness and we approve it without further ado. This information, in some cases, may not be correct, so we must be attentive to all that passes through our mind incessantly.

Everything that leads us to destruction is within us. We can access all that content through our consciousness, even if it is extensive and we have difficulties in detecting all those elements.

If we do not pay attention, we can let ourselves be led by the deception of all those thoughts that are released in that inner speech that slowly seduces us and makes us have a wrong vision of the world.

FOCUS OF ATTENTION

In reality, it all depends on where we put our focus of attention. Sometimes we focus on content that wastes our time and does not lead us to anything useful. If we manage to realize this, we can focus only on those elements that are really useful to us because they are beneficial.

This kind of exercise will later have a consequence on the way we behave. We must remember that everything that we manifest on the outside, is first expressed in our consciousness.

If we manage to correct and moderate what appears in our mind, then it will have a result in our lifestyle and in all those actions we perform.

That is why it is important to be aware of the kind of contents that usually occupy our consciousness, because depending on the direction they take, they will lead us in one way or another.

All those thoughts previous to our behaviors, are also part of our internal dialogue, they are the ones that feed, in some way, our inner voice. We only have to be attentive to it to detect them and thus know the sense and direction to which they point. It is simply a matter of observing and paying attention to this process that occurs constantly and repetitively.

How to achieve it

It may be difficult for us to direct our focus of attention to a specific point voluntarily. We are not used to this way of functioning in which we take command of our own mental functioning.

However, with a little patience and practice we can achieve great advances in the control that we can exercise in this area.

We just have to stop for a moment and relax. Then all that stream of thoughts that we have calms down somehow, as if you think at a slower speed. In this way many mental contents stop arising to your consciousness, opening a space between one element and another that allows you to take control by consciously and voluntarily intercalating a specific thought on which you want to put your focus of attention at that moment.

In reality, everything is based on what we put our focus on. If we become aware of it, we can change that focus, we can divert it to a different point if the current one leads us to conflicts, problems and difficulties. We must be aware that, if we want, we can be in control of what happens in our own mind.

It is only a matter of being attentive and having a conscious attitude in everything we do. It is also necessary that we know how to stop, to establish a pause in time, before all those thoughts that circulate in our consciousness end up taking over us.

Results

Once you achieve it, all your mental mechanism is centered in that thought that you have managed to separate from all that maelstrom of contents that in those moments are in your mind.

In this way you can focus for a certain time on an idea or an image or an aspect that may interest you for some reason. You will be able to achieve this for a certain period of time, but later, after a longer period of time, other different thoughts will come to your mind unexpectedly, will catch you and will make you divert your attention to another different point.

Because of this you will change your task and get ready to perform another action different from the one you were doing. By our own nature it is difficult for us to maintain our attention for a long time on the same task, so it is normal that we switch from one action to another according to the thoughts we are having at any given moment.

When this happens, we can clearly see the repercussions of focusing our attention on certain content. We can foresee the consequences of focusing on a specific type of thoughts. This will allow us to anticipate, to know the results before they occur, because we will be aware at all times of everything that is happening inside.

This will make it possible to save us from many problems, because this anticipation that we can have thanks to this conscious observation of our own thoughts, will help us to avoid many mistakes that we have already made previously.

Just by paying attention to that inner voice that constantly repeats itself, we can achieve results. We will understand ourselves much better; we will understand why we often behave in a way that is not consistent with what we are, with what we really think we should have done in each specific situation.

5. Observe

We must have the ability to observe our inner voice, to be attentive. Then little by little it will diminish, it will fade away; that voice will stop expressing itself.

In those moments you will feel somewhat freer, with a certain control over yourself; you will be flooded with clarity, and you will feel a prudent, sane, reflective calm.

When you feel that your thoughts drown you and you cannot leave them, try to observe your inner voice. Perceive how your own thoughts move, how they try to distract you, to cloud your reason; use a little of your mental power and do not let yourself be dominated by the contents that in those moments are in that voice, in that inner speech that evaluates everything.

If we observe it carefully, we will quickly understand that therein lies the origin of everything we end up doing, because everything that arises in our mind, ultimately ends up manifesting itself outside, in our actions and behaviors that we carry out in the context that surrounds us.

We only have to pay a little attention to know the elements that compose it. They are contents that we have stored in our memory, the result of all the information that we have been gathering throughout each and every one of our past experiences.

If we observe carefully, we will see that it moves and sways throughout the length and breadth of our consciousness, without any kind of impediment. The mind is like your temple.

It is only possible to change this voice if you are aware of it and manage to observe it, if you manage to separate yourself from all those repetitive thoughts and turn off for an instant all that unconscious movement of your mind, in the form of impulses that resurface from the deepest part of yourself and take over your attention, which sometimes are so repetitive that in the end they manage to take control of your own will.

In this way they establish their dominion over you, while you remain distracted, unoccupied, without being very conscious of the consequences of these processes going on inside you.

It becomes necessary, therefore, that we put a stop to this in some way, that we do not remain indifferent when our thoughts are deteriorating us. That is why we must discover what that voice that we all have in our head is trying to manifest. We have to observe it to realize how it is elaborating all those contents that we repeat over and over again.

When we do not find a way out, we must observe it. Then we will become aware of all those mental manifestations that have taken over us, so that they are leading us down a path in which we find ourselves disoriented.

Only if we are sufficiently observant, we can become aware of that movement that confuses us and that with the passage of time is sinking us without any opposition on our part.

Knowing everything that spreads in our mind, we tame in some way that inner voice that is trapping all the manifestations of our consciousness repeatedly.

It is important that we observe that inner voice, that inner speech that, if we allow it, can flood us with toxic and irrational contents; it will be the best way to protect us from the influence of our own mind.

We simply need to appreciate all this by observing the confusion that sometimes exists inside, which is cultivated through that inner voice that little by little pushes us to think in a certain way.

The only way to regulate all these automatic behaviors is by observing ourselves, being curious to know what mechanism is hidden behind all these mechanical actions that we repeat over and over again, as if we were installed in a vicious circle in which we remain for long periods of time because we do not know how to moderate ourselves.

Only if we stay awake and observe this mechanism, we can manage to abandon it; we can stop it in some way.

Only if we observe ourselves and try to establish a certain moderation over this mechanism that we habitually obey without realizing it, we will be able to distinguish our true purpose and all our actions will be inclined towards it.

Only from observation, through serenity, we can order our own mind, unite that which is separated. We can come to clarify many confusions to which we are subjected that overshadow our way of seeing the world.

To follow the mind is to deviate from ourselves; it

is to forget who we are. If we separate ourselves from our true identity, from our authentic personality, there will be no coherence.

We will have an infinity of behaviors, but they will have nothing to do with what we would really like to do, because they will simply be actions that will be derived from the obedience that we maintain towards all those contents that are manifested in our own mind.

PERCEIVING WHAT WE THINK

This voice is frequent and can arise at any time of the day, depending on the activity we are doing. In it we can discover all those reasonings that we make when we try to interpret what is happening to us.

At that moment, when we try to organize the information that comes to us from outside to try to understand the reality we are experiencing, we can easily perceive what we think.

We will clearly appreciate the elements that are present in that instant, in our consciousness. We can see how they accumulate; how they unite with similar contents trying to create structures of thoughts that are arranging our way of seeing the world.

We will be aware of our internal machinery, of that mechanism that we all carry inside and that sometimes establishes a disorder in our internal world that influences our own emotions, our personality and the way we see the world around us.

If we do not know this, many of our reasonings, of our judgments, will be nothing more than the fruit of all those unconscious thoughts that are repeated mechanically in our mind; they will not be the result of a conscious reflection on our part.

If we pay attention to what we think, we can somehow stop many negative reasonings that we have been inserting over time, that we have nurtured without knowing it, without being aware of the consequences that this can bring us.

In our mind there are all kinds of thoughts, while we recreate ourselves in them. They are impressions that emerge from our memory and that we can contemplate, noticing how they are associated with other similar ones. Sometimes they rob us of our calm, they provoke a restlessness that slowly makes us despair, confusing us.

If we do not allow them to rush, to crowd one after the other in our mind, we will be able to voluntarily examine in more detail all that we are thinking at a given moment, under a specific circumstance.

This will help us not to get carried away by the daze, to orient ourselves in a more effective way, putting order to all that confusion that often makes us lose the sense and direction of our actions, which should only be directed towards our true purpose: towards what we really have to do to live in a coherent way.

CLARIFYING MANY DIFFICULTIES

When we abandon ourselves to what is created in our own mind, we lose the link with ourselves. We begin to pay attention to other kinds of content that have nothing to do with who we are, or what we really want to be.

Many of the thoughts that are transmitted in our mind and that remain there for long periods of time, have nothing to do with who we are, with what our true purpose is. If we pay too much attention to them, we will be making a mistake, because we will be allowing ourselves to be dissuaded by a series of thoughts that in many occasions do not adjust to what we really are.

If we have the opportunity to examine them carefully, we will realize how this process takes place, which in the end ends up influencing our own judgments and reasoning.

We will become aware of all those impressions that stir and move throughout our consciousness, how they manifest themselves and the way they influence and subordinate us. We cannot suppress them if we do not become aware of this process that acts in a mechanical way.

If we remain indifferent to all these mental mechanisms, sometimes adverse, we will fall into confusion and disorder on many occasions.

If we explore our inner self a little, we will be able to clarify many difficulties that we create for ourselves on a mental level. With a little willpower on our part, we will manage, in this sense, not to let ourselves be surprised by our own thoughts.

We will avoid, in this way, that suffering is built within our own mind. We will pass from darkness to light, discovering a world that is hidden inside, that does not become visible until we do not silence our mind: that voice, often irrational, that repeats itself over and over again trying to lead us, guiding us in a certain direction.

THREADING TOGETHER WHAT IS UNRAVELED

If I examine my thoughts, I understand what is happening to me, my judgments lead me to understand it clearly. I can know where my worries come from; how suffering develops through all those impressions that spring up in my mind and move back and forth energetically through my consciousness.

If I observe myself, I can recognize what is the inclination of my thoughts in those moments. If I look carefully, I can see how they are born, how they emerge from my own unconscious and delimit me from within, condemning me to see only one reality.

If I give myself up to them, they gradually become contaminated, articulating a mental structure from which it is difficult to free myself.

Only if I observe all this, I can escape, get away from this irrational confusion that insists on growing inside me when I let myself be carried away by my own thoughts.

If I observe attentively all this disorder that is represented in my consciousness, I can recognize the details, explore and appreciate what is happening there, in its full extent.

It is an effective means to thread together that which is untidy, that which is disordered. The mind is chaotic, and if we do not try to orient it, even little by little, it can be even more disconcerting.

In order not to let ourselves be distracted by all that it proposes, we must raise our attention and not let ourselves be surprised by all those contents that are emerging, that are being built by joining one with another with a tendency to remain as long as possible.

If we are aware of how they originate, we will return our mind to the true reasoning, to have a coherent discourse again.

THE OBJECTIVE

Our inner voice makes us experience different sensations, depending on the thoughts that are taking place in our mind at that moment. If we recognize and examine them, we will not allow ourselves to be absorbed by their influence. We will have the advantage that we can exercise control over them, thus having the opportunity to let them pass without further ado.

That should be our goal when we observe ourselves, and more specifically when we perceive all those thoughts that are released in our inner voice and that are in our mind coming from our memory.

In this way we will recover the tranquility and sobriety that can only be achieved when we move away from confusion and clarity floods us internally. When we find that calmness that takes us away from suffering and all those irrational thoughts that occupy our consciousness, we move away from the deception of the mind.

In this way we can manage in a more adequate way all those contents that are in it.

TO ATTAIN KNOWLEDGE

If you carefully examine everything around you, you will come to the knowledge of the reality that surrounds you, you will be able to penetrate all its secrets and get to the essence of things, to what is truly important behind all those appearances that are presented outside.

If you are an observer, you will find all the explanations, you only need to contemplate reality, what is happening before you.

It is about inspecting, constantly, what is around you to capture in this way all the wealth of content that is hidden and that many times we do not take into consideration, because we are indifferent to all those little details that are hidden in everything we observe.

With experience and practice we will reach the true knowledge, the origin where everything begins to develop. So, thanks to our own observation, we will be able to transform ourselves. Thanks to our own experience and all that information that we have accumulated over time, which allows us to interpret the world in a reasonable way, away from the fiction of our own imagination, which in many cases is not authentic, because it is often created through fantasies that have nothing to do with reality itself; that we feed without realizing it, holding wrong thoughts that occur again and again in our own consciousness.

If we become accustomed to observe reality, putting aside all those stimuli that distract us and prevent us from seeing the truth of things, we can get to the essence of that which manifests itself before us.

We will focus more on the details and we will elaborate an interpretation of the world closer to what each thing is, to the true reality.

We will create a filter to separate everything that has nothing to do with what we really are, so that we will orient ourselves through life in a more coherent way;

so that this inner voice, which constantly murmurs to us, will spread inside without destroying us, because it will be based on more reasonable thoughts, on judgments closer to the truth and away from the deception of our own imagination, which often limits us, because it is based on fantasies and illusions that have nothing to do with the reality that surrounds us.

All this is possible if we stop in time, if we are observant, if we are attentive to everything that arises in our mind. If we achieve this, we will obtain great benefits.

When I observe my mind, a mysterious world opens up before me. I can become aware of serenity, of what tries to dominate me, of the obstacles that prevent me from seeing clearly the world and the life around me.

I become aware of how my thoughts are grouped together, especially those that are similar. I can perceive how others are shut down if I do not attend to them, when I establish a pause, through silence.

LET IT GO

We just need to observe what is occupying our mind at a particular moment. When we achieve this, we can then analyze if what is occupying our mind at that moment is beneficial or not.

If it is harmful, we have the possibility of letting it pass, not dwelling on it for too long. This is how we can exercise a certain control over that inner voice that at every step is proposing a series of ideas for us to put all our attention on them.

Our mind never stops, we cannot stop thinking. Mental contents are always arising in our consciousness; it is as if we cannot do anything to avoid them. We can pay attention to them, observe them, and in certain cases, with a little willpower on our part, we can also let them pass.

This is the only way that they do not affect us too much, especially if they are negative contents or thoughts that can create an inner discomfort that does not benefit us.

It all depends on where we focus our attention. If we do it on contents that are harmful, or that do not cause us any good, we can self-destruct without knowing it, only because we pay attention to those specific contents and not to others that may be more beneficial. Everything depends on the vision we have of things, of what happens to us, of the thoughts we have in our mind at any given moment.

In fact, everything depends on the importance that we give to each thing that happens to us and to each element that we have in our consciousness. If we focus on a point and we do not separate ourselves from that point, it becomes bigger and bigger, it becomes united with other similar elements, until they become intertwined in such a way that with time they are difficult to eliminate.

MEDITATION

Through meditation we can also observe that inner voice, which whispers a story that sometimes may be true and sometimes not.

Thanks to this state of continuous observation that is meditation, we can dedicate some time to that voice. We can see how it expresses itself, how it manifests itself and how it passes through our consciousness. In such a situation, if we pay attention, we can even reflect on what it is trying to tell us.

Through meditation, through this observation that one can make to oneself, one can appreciate a series of processes that, if we do not remedy them, are perpetuated in time. If they do not find opposition from our part, they do not diminish, they lengthen until they finally make us live in a permanent confusion.

Only in these cases, this inner voice, does not affect us, does not manage to determine us, because we will be aware of its existence and therefore in those moments it stops influencing, contaminating us. We will see that it will slowly stop rushing. It will be disarticulated little by little, as we observe it. All this succession of thoughts will diminish.

If we separate ourselves a little from this mechanism that always accompanies us, we will be able to observe all this movement that occurs in our mind, where all these thoughts are reproduced.

If we are aware of them, we can glimpse the consequences that these kinds of contents may have in the future. Then we can rectify, stop them in some way.

6. Mind

I have always been interested in the secrets hidden in our own mind, I believe that we have enough capacity to discover many of the enigmas that are hidden.

We only have to show a certain interest on our part, when it comes to investigate in all that inner universe that we carry inside and that is composed of a series of elements and processes that work in a continuous way; that in many occasions lead us to confusion, because they are agitated in such a hasty way that in many moments we lose the control of all those automatisms and impulses.

I have always tried to test my own reasoning, the way I have of interpreting the world, everything that happens to me through my own experiences.

I also try to observe my behaviors, which sometimes are born from thoughtless ideas that take hold of me, leading me to a series of somewhat hasty and impulsive actions, which I may later regret when I become aware of what I am doing.

I have always been curious to know the mechanism behind this way of behaving.

CONTENTS

The contents of the mind have their expression in that inner voice that we usually listen to and that contains all those thoughts that occupy a space in our consciousness, and that become strong there, as time goes by. They become resistant, solid to change, so that they are repeated over and over again like a never-ending current; and they expand as time goes by.

We can perceive it in that internal dialogue that we often have with ourselves. There we can discover all those elements that circulate in our mind and that in certain occasions can be pernicious, when they are negative contents that come linked to a pessimistic vision of life.

In our mind, therefore, all those processes that then end up influencing us and guide us, marking the path we should follow, are schemed. They are elements that we have been acquiring through experience and that have been stored in our memory, in such a way that they remain there, until a stimulus makes them move and arise in our mind, capturing our attention.

HIDDEN QUALITIES

This is how our mind works. We can leave it to its free will, let it be the one that proposes us what we should think at every moment; or we can exercise control over this internal mechanism, so that we can change all those automatic processes that lead us to always have the same thoughts over and over again.

If we do it this way we will find a great number of qualities that are hidden behind all that amalgam of thoughts that, by occupying all the space, somehow hide many hidden capacities that do not come to light because our automatic mental processes occupy all the protagonism and all the space of our consciousness.

If we allow this, we will never be able to look beyond and we will never discover what is behind all those thoughts, that mental noise that traps us and does not allow us to look beyond.

To get to know yourself -to get to know how you really are-, to know what your best qualities are, it is necessary that you transcend your own thoughts, that you are above everything that your mind is proposing to you at every step.

If you manage to take that leap, you will be able to discover that other dimension where you find yourself, beyond your own thoughts. Then you will know yourself and you will know what you really are; since what your mind says you are, is based on information from the past, which is information that comes from previous experience, which does not have to be true, since at the time you elaborated it with the interpretations you made of what happened to you under certain circumstances. And your own interpretations about reality and yourself, may not always be true, because somehow they are still subjective, because you are the one who creates them and in the end they may not be more than a set of misleading beliefs that are marking your vision of reality, your vision of the world, so that cause you to behave in a certain way, under certain circumstances, because in the end you just follow the information taken from each and every one of your past experiences.

MENTAL PROGRAMMING

Thanks to reflection and observation of myself I have come to the conclusion that, in many moments throughout the day, we function automatically, we loosen our own will and extend our actions following a series of mechanical instructions that our own mind dictates to us.

In reality, these are activities that we have previously programmed through the constant repetition of actions that we have turned into a habit over time; in such a way that when we put all these previously programmed behaviors into practice, we are reinforcing them, we are extending that programming so that later we return again to repeat those same actions when we find ourselves in similar circumstances.

In such cases we limit ourselves to follow a program that in the end ends up taking over us, because we are subject to that process, we abandon ourselves to it as if we were subordinated to that mechanism and we did not have the capacity at that moment to take the initiative.

At this point, it is important that we become aware of these unconscious movements, since there are mental programming that are not beneficial, because they make us spend a lot of energy in activities that are of little use. It is clear that we can acquire habits that can deteriorate us over time, without us being very aware of it.

Mechanical action

Many times we act in a mechanical way, without

worrying too much about what we are doing. All those behaviors that we repeat cannot be diminished so easily, since they are part of a programming that we have been nurturing over time. We have become accustomed to it until it has become a habit, and from then on we do everything automatically.

To change this habit we must introduce some change in the chain. We have to know, first, if it is harmful to us, if it is necessary to change. In such a case it is necessary to introduce new behaviors so that the existing ones are reduced and disappear. It is a matter of exchanging some behaviors for others until a new programming is established that in the end leads to a new habit.

If we dig a little deeper, we will realize that the mental programming that we are trying to modify is the result of all those manifestations that are repeated in our mind. They have remained there for so long that they have finally managed to establish a link with our own actions: we have transformed them into behaviors that we have frequently repeated until they have become a habit.

REPEAT

Our own mind's habitual way of acting is based on the repetition, almost always, of the same contents, of the same thoughts. This entails an expenditure of energy that makes us always be attentive to the same elements. This in turn causes us to have that feeling of being constantly stuck in the same place, that we do not move forward, since in the end we end up always thinking about the same ideas, the same thoughts, and we will not have that feeling that we are moving in a certain direction.

Only if we manage to stop this gear -this mechanism-, we can give it a determined sense; we can reach a concrete end, through a specific direction. But in order to do so, we must first introduce ourselves into this mechanism, including a thought different from those that are already there, within this chain of thoughts that are constantly repeated.

Once we manage to introduce it in that chain, in the end it becomes much easier to change the orientation of all that we hear in that inner voice that does not cease.

What we think about throughout the day, in most cases, is usually always the same. We are always centered on the same ideas, which are grouped together and that in the end end guide us, lead us, making us have a certain vision on some issues about the life around us, our experiences or our relationships with others.

IT IS DYNAMIC

In reality, many forms of thought are created through small fragments, through brief reflections that we make about those things that happen to us and that are joined one with the other, until they manage to extend in time.

In this way our own mental structure is established, which ultimately is the one that leads us, it is the one that shows us the way we should go.

This mental structure is created on the basis of a series of similar thoughts that have been united because we have repeated them in a continuous way; they have been linked to each other in such a way that in the end they have been shaping our own reasoning, our way of understanding the world and the reality that surrounds us.

Over time it develops, we increase it with new thoughts. When we realize that some of the contents of this structure are no longer valid, we replace them with new ones.

Therefore, we could say that our way of seeing reality and understanding the world around us changes over time, so our way of thinking has a dynamic character.

Sometimes we are interested in thinking in a particular way about a particular issue; and at other times we may find it more useful to think in a different way, sometimes even in the opposite way. It all depends on what interests us at any given moment.

That is why we can often change our opinion, depending on the situation or the circumstances in which we find ourselves at any given moment.

Our mind is dynamic, it does not always remain fixed in the same contents, it varies in real time, depending on the experiences that are taking place in each situation.

All these changes influence our reasoning, the interpretations we make of what happens to us. This can cause great confusion at times: it can lead to contradictory thoughts, so that in the same period of time we can come to believe in one idea and in its opposite; we can think that what is happening to us is wonderful, but in a short period of time we can come to believe the opposite.

These abrupt changes are also part of our mental structure, which tries to adapt itself to the circumstances we are living in each moment, it is changing, so to speak, depending on the usefulness for us of the thoughts of which it is composed.

There is a total dependence on our mind for everything we do. Rarely are we freed from it. It is important for everything we end up doing. We cannot suppress it so easily. It is the one that marks the direction to follow and also the one that often paralyzes us, if a set of negative thoughts come together in it and end up dominating us.

INFORMATION FROM THE PAST

Our vision of life is limited to all that accumulated information from the past that we have been acquiring throughout our experiences, from all those events that we have had the opportunity to experience and live; from the results of our own actions…

All this influences our way of being, our way of facing the world and our way of seeing the reality that surrounds us.

In truth, all our mental contents are nothing more than the fruit of our past, of all the information we have accumulated over time.

Whether it is positive or negative, all these contents are stored in our memory and little by little they emerge in our mind in relation to what we are doing at any given moment; and they influence and determine us; and they direct and condition us, influencing the decisions we must take in certain circumstances.

All this actually shapes who we are, it is part of ourselves, because it is something that we have so internalized that makes us be in a certain way; although we can transcend all this, being aware that it is a part of us.

PROJECTION

What we do on a daily basis gives us a great deal of information about how we feel inside. Everything we do outside is a manifestation of the kind of activity that is in our own mind.

If inside we are at peace, our actions will have a parsimony that will be visible to the eyes of others. If within us there is calmness, we will also manifest it outside. It will appear clearly when we express ourselves; in the way we behave; in the way we carry out our own actions…

The inner tranquility will be transferred outside, in our way of being in the world; and others will perceive it very quickly.

That which dwells within us we externalize outside, and many of the things that we observe in the external world are installed in our memory, are sedimented and then are placed in our mind, often unconsciously, in such a way that many times they direct our thoughts and influence our own actions.

Everything that we sow in our mind is then manifested in our behaviors. We can clearly distinguish it in everything we do, in every action we perform. Our actions are nothing more than the external manifestations of that which dominates us internally at every moment.

Thoughts are the foundation, the basis of our actions. If our thoughts are not healthy, what we do on the outside will not be healthy either. If discouragement reigns in our mind, due to a series of thoughts that go in that direction, this will also be transferred outside. All those around us will be able to observe it clearly in the way we stand before them, in our attitude and in the mood they can perceive in us.

Therefore, we can say that everything that is elaborated in our mind is then projected outside, in the world around us. It is externalized in our actions, so we cannot hide anything of what we carry inside, because somehow, sooner or later, it will end up manifesting itself outside and others will have the opportunity to detect it.

It is enough for us to observe the behavior of others to realize how they think, how their judgments and reasoning are. We can immediately detect the ideas they have about the world, about life and about others; if there is negativity in them or if, on the other hand, they are positive people. Through their comments we can glimpse many of their beliefs, their points of view about some topics, because many of the contents that become strong in our mind end up manifesting themselves on the outside, in one way or another.

Most of the time we limit ourselves to extending outside what we carry inside. We abandon ourselves to the ideas that arise in our mind, without stopping to carry out a recognition, a previous analysis. We allow our mind to elaborate a whole series of judgments and reasonings about any subject, without being aware that all these contents can later see the light, can manifest themselves outside, when we relate to others. They can come out of us through any comment we make on any particular subject. We will realize that what was hidden in the end is discovered, it comes to light.

That is how the mechanism works. In the end we end up following an idea that is nothing more than the fruit of accumulated information from the past. That idea sometimes translates into a specific behavior on our part that others can clearly observe. That specific action is nothing more than the fruit of our own thoughts, of those that have managed to reach a privileged position in that infinite space that is our consciousness.

ESTABLISHING AN ORDER

For me the mind is a labyrinth. To move through it it is necessary to delimit it, if you do not do it, it can exhaust you, weaken you.

Depending on the direction you choose, you can make the labyrinth even bigger, or you can solve it. The latter only happens if you manage to put the pieces in order, if you recognize all the elements that appear in it. If you understand how it is composed and remain attentive to everything that emerges from it, exploring it in detail, you can solve its enigmas.

To do this it is necessary, first of all, to establish an order. Separate a series of elements and all those contents that are shown there, almost impulsively. It is a matter of clarifying all that space, being aware of all those representations that arise from the bottom of your memory and that in many occasions are toxic.

Once you observe them, you will see how they fade away at the same time. All that stream of absurd thoughts that often occupies our consciousness will begin to shrink. All that structure created by all those contents that manage to capture your attention in such a way that in the end they end up influencing your own decisions will be disunited.

TAKING CONTROL OF THE REINS

To take control of our own mind is not so simple. The mind governs us most of the time, so we are forced to break that chain of thoughts that are repeated over and over again, to intersperse the thoughts we want, the contents on which we really want to focus.

We must break, therefore, the inertia of our own mind to introduce ourselves in that mechanism, and from there impose the contents to which we want to pay attention.

This can only be done through continuous practice. The normal thing is that we let ourselves be carried away by everything that our mind proposes to us; but it is worth trying, because if we do it, in the end, we will gain control of this process that occurs in a mechanical and repetitive way, so that in many occasions we are not aware that this is happening inside us.

The advantage of acting in this way, intervening in our mental processes, is that we can change the course of our own thoughts, the direction of our mind. We can achieve a mental control that makes us focus on what we really want or what we need.

Being conscious

Our mind is a mechanism that does not stop, that is not interrupted. To deactivate it, all we need to do is to be aware of our own thoughts. This is the only way for our mind to stabilize and put an end to that wheel of continuous thoughts that never seems to end.

When this happens, it is as if we take control of what is in our inner world; it is as if we gain control of our own mind. In such a way that, if we reach that point, it is we ourselves who, through our own initiative, can decide where we put our focus of attention; who can choose the kind of thoughts we are going to prioritize.

In this way we can come to give a certain orientation for our mind to run in a particular direction. We would no longer be acting, in this case, in an automatic and unconscious way. At that moment we have the command, the control of our thoughts.

Once this happens, we can create new ideas, we can consciously join some thoughts with others, thus creating a new mental structure different from the one that was already established before.

Benefits

When we achieve this new change, we will observe that we begin to have a new vision of things; a more objective vision of the world and of ourselves, since we will be functioning under a conscious mental structure and, therefore, our vision of things and of the world will be much closer to reality, to the truth.

This will contribute, to some extent, to our personal development, because we will have a new way of being in the world, much more conscious. So everything we do will have a greater coherence and will be more in line with who we really are, with our true purpose,

with our true self, which is in the deepest part of ourselves, away from the influence of the thoughts of the
mind.

7. Mental conflict

Sometimes my mind is occupied by ideas that I cannot let go of. They are crazy thoughts that come into my head and that I find difficult to moderate. If I remain attentive to them for too long, my state of mind darkens, while I let myself be carried away by all that is unleashed inside and from which I cannot manage to escape.

In some moments I feel confused. For brief instants an accumulation of problems begins in me, at the same time that I feel the need to solve them in an urgent way. This paralyzes me, I can't find enough tranquility to form a rough idea of the direction my thoughts are taking at that moment.

It is not pleasant to feel chained to all those circumstances that cause a disturbance in my mood. I always try to appease any tension that comes from some anomaly, but I do not always find the necessary attitude to tame my thoughts and thus suppress all those toxic contents that take over my mind and try to envelop me and isolate me from reality.

Sometimes I feel a tightness in my chest, which has its origin in all those conflicts that sometimes pile up inside me. Whenever I experience this sensation, I understand perfectly well the cause that originates it. I know that part of my bodily well-being emanates from everything that takes place in my mind.

If I allow conflicts to precipitate in my mind, this will end up manifesting in one way or another in my own body: in the agitation, in the nervousness that I may feel, in all that anxiety that slowly shrinks me inside and that little by little weakens me.

PROBLEMS

When you think that everything is collapsing and you feel dejected, on the verge of disaster, hurry to face all the confusion that you are experiencing at that moment.

You must find out, first of all, what it is that is producing this alteration in you. It may be that the cause is to be found in your own decisions, which may have been incorrect; or it may all come from your own reasoning, which is irrational and perhaps you are creating a gigantic ball of something that has no reason to be.

In any case, it is always advisable to explore the causes behind the disillusionment that is discouraging you at that moment. You must regain hope as soon as possible. You cannot stay there, without doing anything, you have to compose again that which is disordered inside you, to see which thoughts are disproportionate, unrealistic.

You have to become the moderator of yourself, not to let yourself be carried away by all those exaggerated confusions that in many moments you create in your own mind, that lead you to despondency, influencing your own moods.

To put an end to all that which causes you restlessness, you must give yourself a pause. In this way you will see things in a more lucid way, with greater clarity. You will estimate the reality in a more objective way, and the decisions that you take in this respect will adjust in a more faithful way to the reality of what in those moments is happening.

If we do not repair that which causes us suffering and we do not worry about it, in the end the damage will become greater, the misfortune will end up taking over us, in such a way that it will extend over time, until we decide to remedy all those setbacks that are confusing us.

In reality, we are the administrators of our moods, we cannot turn our attention away from that which is spreading inside. If it is harmful, we have to dissolve it in time, not allowing it to expand and degrade us.

When a wave of negativity settles in our mind, it gradually influences our own emotions, trying to stay there as long as possible, so it is necessary to restore the balance by re-interpreting the situation we are going through at that moment.

All this is achieved thanks to the exploration that we can do if we observe what is upsetting us, what is trying to steal our serenity. It is the only way to reorient our life towards our true purpose, towards our authentic path.

With a little strength on our part we can achieve this, we can get back on the right direction. In this way we will continue to grow while maintaining our balance, without getting carried away by our impulsive mind, where most of our problems originate.

DO NOT EXPIRE WITH TIME

Everything that flows in our mind can be positive or negative, it depends on the contents that we feed with our attention and through the repetition of those elements.

They are fragments that are linked to each other, depending on the importance we give them. Some may be transitory, and others may remain for long periods of time, if they manage to establish themselves in our mind in a continuous and repetitive way.

The problem is that they do not expire with time. If we become obsessed with maintaining the same line of thought, the only thing we achieve is to maintain over time a series of ideas that end up trapping us, making us see a different, unstable reality.

All these thoughts are perpetuated to the extent that we transform them into actions, to the extent that we do not resist or reject them.

If there is no reaction on our part, these contents will be reinforced, because they will not find any obstacle, any difficulty to continue to concur.

Our mind will eventually become a tendency from which we will not be able to separate so easily, since this kind of thoughts will end up dominating us, constantly enveloping us through that inner voice that is directing our own decisions, accompanying us at every step, associating all those contents that suddenly arise in our mind.

WE ALLOW OURSELVES TO BE ENVELO-PED

A great part of our mental disorders originate through this mechanism. In many occasions we abandon ourselves to judgments and reasonings that have no consistency. We do it because we have granted them an excessive importance and for that reason they end up repeating constantly in our mind, absorbing us, capturing our attention. In such a way that our reflections end up contaminated by these contents, until we end up creating a mistaken vision of reality, which remains for long periods of time because of so much repetition.

And all this is because we allow ourselves to be enveloped, imprisoned, by all that our mind is proposing to us at every moment. We must be aware that we can direct these processes, take control and make the appropriate modifications so that our thoughts and actions go in the right direction.

We cannot entrust everything to what the mind proposes to us, since many times this one feeds on unconscious contents without any foundation, which in the end take possession of our own judgments. They flood us with wrong impressions that little by little damage us, while they repeat themselves in our mind until they end up dominating us, forcing us to act in a concrete sense.

All these mental manifestations determine us, forcing us to act in a definite way, without any order or control on our part. This is the reason why we often do not find explanations for what we do.

And it is because we act unconsciously for most of

the time, limiting ourselves to follow the dictates of our own thoughts, which supply us with the actions we must perform in each circumstance.

WE LIVE IN DISORDER

Most of the time we live in disorder, separated from ourselves, from what we really are, abandoned to the fate of all those thoughts that are released in our mind.

Our mistakes and errors come from there, from that lack of awareness that allows many irrational thoughts to take over us, our mind.

Most of the time we function this way, without stopping to make a detailed analysis of all that happens in our consciousness. We let ourselves be carried away by the disorder, without exercising control, without exploring, without at least recognizing what we are thinking at a given moment. We allow it to develop without further ado, to unfold throughout our mind and to extend in time, to invade us and in the end to dominate us, taking over our will.

We don't realize that it all starts there; we don't discover it until we suffer the consequences. Then it is when we look at our judgments, to discover those that are proving harmful to us; to try to abandon them or replace them with others.

We are the ones who, in the end, can make that choice; or we can let ourselves be dragged down by everything that tries to separate us from who we are. We can reconstruct our way of thinking, order our ideas a little, expel that which torments us, not allowing it to extend any longer in our consciousness.

To achieve this, we must be attentive to our inner

voice, to that inner dialogue that we all have with ourselves where all those mental contents that try to show
us the path we should follow are manifested.

With a little willpower on our part, we can separate
ourselves, deviate from that voice, free ourselves from
it, as long as we stay awake, attentive to all that is reproduced in our mind.

CREATION OF DIFFICULTIES

Many times problems originate from within. Many
difficulties are created by ourselves, when we do not
know how to select the best decisions or do not seek a
balance in our actions.

We can be for a long time feeding our own mistakes, without being very conscious of it. Only when the
situation begins to overwhelm us do we easily realize
the obstacles that are hindering our path; many of
which we have created when we have been obstinate
in following a direction that was not the most beneficial.

Many times we make mistakes in our actions, so
that we follow a path that is not really in line with who
we really are, it does not fit our true purpose.

When we reach a certain point, we realize that we
have to change direction, that we cannot stay on that
path, so we have to turn our attention to other ideas,
to other kinds of different thoughts.

Some people perceive this very quickly; others, on
the other hand, do not stop to observe themselves, to
look for an explanation of what they are doing. They
are not aware of the direction their life is taking.

If we direct our gaze towards our inner world, we

can solve many of the difficulties to which we are subjected, some of which we create when we do not know how to correctly compose reality: that which manifests itself in front of us, which is visible to our eyes, but which we later interpret, sometimes, in a way that is separate and far from the truth.

External information

The information that we have acquired outside, in some way predetermines us, it is slowly introduced in our conscience, it fills us with a certain information that in the end becomes the domain of our own thoughts, of our reasoning and of all those beliefs that little by little we are elaborating.

It is essential that we are also attentive to all that information that comes to us from outside, the result of our interaction with the external world; it can provide us with a benefit, or it can cause confusion to spread even further.

Everything that enters through our senses can lead us to see life from a negative point of view, depending on where it comes from. It can bring us closer to our own happiness; or it can push us away, causing restlessness. It can hold us back, creating a problem in our own mind.

REALIZING

We simply give ourselves to what our mind disposes in each moment and we let ourselves be guided, dragged, without previously analyzing if what we are doing has a concrete purpose.

Only with the passage of time, when we suffer the consequences of our behaviors, we become aware of the importance of having acted in a certain sense, of having accepted without further ado everything that was proposed to us at the time.

Only when there is imbalance, only when we suffer suffering and confusion, we become aware of the mistakes we have made and there is a disposition to change, to eliminate all those mental representations that are causing us harm.

This is our habitual way of behaving. This is our inner workings. What is created in our mind is transmitted in such a way that in the end we end up turning it into a concrete action, which may or may not be beneficial.

Depending on the importance we attach to it, we will repeat it over time and this will make it become a habit, which will later be difficult to eradicate in case we consider it necessary, in case it does not bring us anything.

When we are conscious it seems that our conflicts diminish, since all those thoughts that are part of them begin to separate, to disintegrate, and all those disorders that confuse us stop dominating us, so that other more positive thoughts begin to occupy our conscience.

All this is possible if you observe carefully. It is possible to abandon this process, to interrupt it, if you pay a little attention to this inner voice that tries to convince you through a series of reasonings that are disordered, that lead you to uneasiness, to worry.

AVOID CONFUSION

It is important to pay attention to all this that is produced in our inner world, since it is the best way to clarify our mind, to eliminate that which produces confusion, which has no coherent logic and whose only purpose is to waste our limited energy.

When we are victims of despondency and we need to expel everything that is hurting us inside, we must be attentive and watch that inner voice, because it is undoubtedly what is guiding us at that moment towards destruction, it is what is preventing us from finding the clarity to find the correct representations that lead us to distinguish reality in an objective way.

We cannot allow it to spread, originating the restlessness for a longer period of time. If we give it continuity, as if it were just another mechanism, it will spread a discourse that will guide us, that will mark our path without us being very conscious of it.

To prevent our voice from leading us to this situation, we must be attentive to the quality of our own thoughts. In this way we will know if what we are thinking at that moment is beneficial or not.

We can anticipate, in this way, to see the consequences that can have a certain way of thinking. We only have to look at our mood, at the kind of emotions we experience when we focus on a particular thought; at what we feel when we focus on certain ideas.

In this way we can anticipate the possible consequences of all those contents that arise in our mind. It is only necessary that we are aware and put our focus of attention on these contents. This is the best way to avoid being dominated by our own thoughts and by everything that appears in our consciousness.

If we pay attention to all that exists within our inner world, we can have more facilities to organize, to protect ourselves from all those toxic contents that want to absorb us.

NOT AVOIDING OURSELVES

If we move away from ourselves, if we evade ourselves in everything that our mind proposes to us, we can hurt ourselves without being aware of it, because we can stop in inadequate contents that can cause us an internal imbalance, with the danger that this entails, because all this makes us wander in uncertainty, makes us lose our calm: that inner peace that is like a door that invites us to enter beyond, in that other dimension where our mind does not have so much influence, because thoughts hardly intervene; in that other space where silence is cultivated and there are not too many components that can distract us, where there is no tension and neither suffering.

ANALYZE

If we stop to evaluate, we will realize where our own suffering comes from, from the kind of negative thoughts that make us consider the world differently. We will realize how we let ourselves go; how our mind is shaping us through all that collection of information that we usually do in our memory, in which all our knowledge is stored, all that wisdom that we have been saving and that we have acquired through all those impressions that have been coming to us from the outside. If we dig a little, we will realize that we treasure all that information.

All these contents remain hidden, disorganized, because they are very abundant. They are all those elements that appear in our reflections, in our mental manifestations; some of which affect us, if they are loaded with a very intense emotion. Then they influence our mood: we can go from joy to sadness very quickly for this reason.

All this information is stored inside and we cannot replace it with another; only with time and with a little observation on our part, we can try to divert those elements that do not benefit us, that are negative or that create inner discomfort; but we can only achieve this if we become aware.

When there are obstacles, we must analyze, even briefly, what is causing them; see what we are giving importance to in those moments. Surely there will be the reason for all those difficulties that we often encounter and that extend for long periods of time without us being able to find a solution to banish them.

We must analyze a little the composition of those contents that are reproduced in our mind. We can observe, discover how they are divided, how they reproduce.

Then we will be able to realize how they are elaborated, which are the most habitual and how they influence our own actions. In reality, we are the ones who praise them, although in the end they end up directing us if we lose control over this mechanism.

Most of them are in our mind, we just have to explore a little to clarify all those confusions that we make without realizing it.

Through practice we can resolve all those mental conflicts that lead us to pessimism and sadness. We can avoid associating some contents with others, until in the end all those elements stop manifesting in our consciousness. In this way we will become more resistant to all that suffering that runs through our mind and that is found in many thoughts that we have daily.

GO TO THE BEGINNING

What we think is the beginning of everything. If we have enough lucidity to go to the beginning, where we begin to repeat an idea constantly, we will immediately realize the transcendence of this fact. We will perceive that we have reached a point where there is no turning back, where we cannot change our course. This idea continues to advance, spreading throughout our consciousness, until it ends up directing us, leading us to our own behaviors.

We depend on that which manifests itself in our mind, even if it causes us an inner imbalance at times.

All the difficulties, obstacles, mental conflicts, come from there: from that operation in which a series of contents insist on taking control of our own mind, without our participation.

If we have the astuteness to observe it, we will realize that it is there, many times, where our confusion begins: when a series of thoughts come together and become generalized, but we hardly stop to interpret them.

In the end, this ends up transporting us to a vision of things that does not correspond to reality, so it creates division within, while we remain immobile, doing nothing. We only limit ourselves to follow that which in an imprecise way is created in our mind, even if it is far from the truth or unreasonable, or does not have a concrete purpose.

All that which is shown through our mental activity, which forms our judgments about the world around us, little by little captures our attention and does not cease to increase. It limits us, in the sense that we stick only to what we think at that moment, discarding other possibilities.

Our reasoning becomes allied with those contents, in such a way that our judgments run along the same line as what is manifesting in our mind, because in those moments we are as if we were asleep: we are not aware of the influence that all those elements are having on us. We simply let ourselves be carried away by all those representations that try to unite with each other, to associate, forming a set of thoughts, a mental structure that tries to force us to see things in a certain way.

We can avoid everything that deceives us, everything that obstinately tries to make us unhappy. We only have to go to the beginning, where all those false ideas in which we believe without having thought about them for a moment originate.

If we keep our attention, we will become aware of their origin: where they begin; how they are formed; how they take hold of all that inner world that we all carry inside, occupying all that mental space where our beliefs are created and all those judgments and o-pinions that arise when we analyze the reality that surrounds us.

Everything starts there, everything has its origin in what appears in our mind and then becomes our inner dialogue: in those messages that we say to ourselves and that sprout in our mind in an unconscious way.

CLARIFYING THE MIND

Sometimes it is advisable to abandon certain ideas that cause disorder in your mind. Without you being very conscious of it, inside you may be creating a mental structure through a series of confused thoughts. When you try to eliminate or expel them, in some cases it may be very complicated, since they have already established a wall, by force of repetition, which is difficult to tear down.

All these representations that are articulated in your mind, may be causing you harm, preventing your happiness. Therefore it is necessary that you clear your mind, that you learn somehow to direct all those incoherent thoughts that are repeated continuously within you.

It all depends on the importance you give to those contents. It is clear that, if you do not pay attention to them, they stop being distributed throughout your mind, they stop transmitting all the anguish they carry with them.

Your mental structure that is created in you without you realizing it may be eternalized. If you do not become aware of it, it may remain there for a long time, robbing you of your balance, making your reasoning illogical. You can live in ignorance, without knowing what causes all the suffering that you often carry with you.

It is all part of these contents that have grown in your mind without you being very aware of it. If you manage to clarify yourself, to observe carefully all these elements that spread in your consciousness, you will reach an inner peace and a balance that will enrich you, that will become stronger as you gain control of yourself.

BROADEN YOUR VISION

When discouragement arrives and we are on the edge of the precipice and we feel confused for some reason, something that can give us a guarantee is to desist and abandon the thoughts that in those moments we have in our mind.

To do this we must broaden our gaze and concentrate our attention on the contents that are imposing themselves on our consciousness.

In this way we can put an end to them, because as we observe them, they lose their influence and move to another place, through a movement that allows these thoughts to stop grouping.

Once they diminish, a calmness begins to develop to which we are not accustomed. In these cases there is no longer an intention in our mind, because the thoughts that used to occupy it leave a space where there are hardly any images and other elements.

It is for this reason that, in these cases, our restlessness is shortened, because nothing incites us, we do not feel chained to any thought, since those that were there are losing their strength and begin to diminish, to abandon that space of consciousness that they used to occupy before.

With this kind of exercises we can put an end to all that mental confusion that, in many cases, remains for a long time in our mind without being able to level it.

FREEDOM

When we reach true freedom is when we free ourselves from the limitations of our own mind, when we have the ability to take a step beyond our normal mental activity.

Only then can we experience the dissolution of our emotional conflicts. This experience can only be obtained if we get away from the noise of the mind, from all that set of repetitive thoughts that are constantly entering our consciousness, in such a way that in many occasions they submerge us in an irrational abyss that fills us with anguish and an inner agitation that we cannot understand.

If we know how to place ourselves in that state of mind where there are hardly any thoughts and we separate ourselves from all those unconscious expressions that little by little determine us, we can reach that sensation of freedom in which we find no obstacle: nothing that can paralyze us, no enemy, no difficulty.

When we have this presentiment, when we perceive this sensation of consciousness, we feel that there is a transformation; as if our mind were less burdened, less occupied.

In such a state everything seems simpler, for in everything there is an order, a direction; as if we function in a different way, with more foundation and reasonableness, with more intelligence, with more reason. Our judgments seem less confused and our understanding less complicated.

In such a situation our inner voice stops pounding us as it usually does. All events occurring outside cease to influence us.

8. Suffering

Suffering and all other ailments arise from mental activity, especially if we give license to all those thoughts that create affliction in the deepest part of ourselves.

It gradually creeps into our mind, through our reason, and begins to generate slowly increasing setbacks as it travels through our consciousness.

This state can persist for a long time, so that in the end it becomes part of that internal conversation we have, where you can clearly see all that disorder, all that convulsion that afflicts us.

If we investigate a little we will realize that everything comes from there, from all those thoughts that arise in our mind that little by little entangle us, in such a way that makes us err in our own vision of reality; when suffering hovers over us it is for this reason.

The origin of our suffering is in our thoughts. If our thoughts are negative, we come to the conviction that the world is also like that, in that way, and all our judgments and reasoning and reflections are configured from that point of view.

Our torment is provoked by the thoughts that are fanned in our mind, that make us feel a drowning that takes us away from that calm that we should have constantly.

If we examine ourselves, we will realize that our suffering is lodged there. We can discover it if we stop a little to observe all that mental clatter that we maintain without knowing it.

We must be aware that everything comes from there, from that mechanism that we all have internally and that makes it possible for thoughts to arise mechanically, unconsciously, and that we allow ourselves to be trapped by them.

Suffering also comes, in some way, from that lack of capacity on our part to discover what is behind all those contents that we see in our consciousness and that try to capture and call our attention, until they manage to disturb us and create a restlessness that little by little compresses us, crushing us, exhausting us.

MECHANISM

There are certain ideas that end up appropriating us if we do not reject them. First we must notice if they are beneficial or not. Some thoughts that lead us directly to suffering, have the capacity to provoke an internal anguish that gains strength as these thoughts are repeated in our consciousness.

Everything that is in our mind can provoke an emotional state that can develop as these contents evolve. It becomes necessary, therefore, to confront this mechanism that confuses us, that many times disconcerts us, making us lose our peace of mind.

All these elements then develop and increase as we pay attention to them. If they are negative, they can lead us to a bottomless abyss, they can incline us to have a pessimistic vision of life and they can even determine what we should do at any given moment.

This mechanism is what is behind our obsessions, because everything that affects us is repeated over and over again in our mind, without us doing anything to avoid it. And it does it in such a way that in the end it ends up affecting us, influencing our mood, our joy.

This is what generates our affliction, our sadness, the fact of giving relevance and allowing some thoughts to end up dominating you, occupying all that mental space that could be occupied by other kinds of more positive thoughts, more beneficial and healthy.

LIVING IN DISORDER

We find it difficult to maintain consistency in our actions. We like to live in disorder, we insist on blindly following the impulses that arise from our unconscious. We let ourselves be carried away by that energy that flows from deep within us, that we do not know how to manage and that leads us to perform a particular action in the context in which we live.

In reality, inside there is a machinery that works constantly and that is marking the direction in which we must go.

On many occasions, this direction, which is already set for us, leads us to suffering. Sometimes, this can become considerable if all those negative thoughts that flourish in our consciousness remain there for a prolonged period of time.

Without being very conscious of it, we can create a world full of adversities, if we do not investigate enough and observe the type of thoughts that are damaging us, that are distorting our vision of the reality and that in some way are determining us; since they are marking the direction that we must follow.

IF WE GET USED TO IT

If we submit and get used to them and we do not realize in time that they are just simple thoughts, a negativism will spread and will develop as these thoughts are repeated in our mind.

If we allow ourselves to be flooded by them, we will be submerged in suffering, in a vision of the world where we will only find setbacks that little by little will crush us, constantly hitting us.

All these elements, in the end, generate restlessness, affliction, through a movement that we must stop to regain our tranquility, to return to normality and regain the calm that puts an end to all confusion.

9. Thoughts

Every day I feed my thoughts with everything I observe, I accumulate information at every step, with everything I do, with everything that appears before me, that penetrates my head.

I tend to focus on what catches my attention. Momentarily, almost without realizing it, my thoughts begin to arise in relation to what I am observing.

If I remain attentive and do not divert my attention to something else, my thoughts are related to other similar thoughts, in such a way that they are chained and remain there, creating impressions related to what I have in front of me at that moment.

Much of what we perceive through the senses becomes the material from which thoughts are made.

To the extent that we remain attentive to an external stimulus, thoughts appear that try to help us understand what we have in front of us. In a way, their function is to look for an explanation that helps us to understand the reality that is manifesting itself outside at any given moment.

They are mental representations that we have acquired over time and that are shown in our mind as we interact in the physical world, externally, in the reality that surrounds us. In this way we solve the different difficulties that we face.

Thanks to what we think, we establish an order in all the information we acquire from outside. If it is relevant, we end up registering it and filing it in our memory. Later, when we find ourselves in a similar situation, it will emerge in our mind, it will manifest itself to help us understand what we are observing.

At that moment we can also realize that many thoughts arise in our mind without us paying attention to something that is outside, in the external world. Many thoughts arise spontaneously, without our having provoked them previously. They appear with a very vigorous energy and move throughout our consciousness, and may have nothing to do with reality or with the circumstances that exist outside at that moment.

They are contents that are also stored in our memory and that rise in our consciousness, many times without a determined direction, without a concrete objective or a clear purpose.

We make room for all kinds of thoughts, whether they are good or not. We cling to them and act accordingly. We do not manage to free ourselves for a moment from all those elements that accumulate in our mind, that crowd our consciousness and slowly captivate us.

We hardly have enough time to reflect on them, to analyze a little the changes they can produce if we give them relevance, if we allow them to control us.

Sometimes they are so numerous that we do not have time to establish an order, to simplify them, to keep only the most convenient ones.

All these thoughts then have a development within

our own consciousness. They increase or decrease depending on the importance we give them, or the time we focus on them.

Sometimes they can easily confuse us, they can lead us to contradictions of which we can later become aware.

THE IMPORTANT

What is important is not what we see, but what we experience inside when we observe what is around us. That which ends up imposing itself in our mind, in relation to what we have in front of us, is what is truly important.

Therefore, we should not divert our attention from what we think about each of our experiences that we are having. Everything that surrounds those experiences is not what is transcendental; where we should focus our attention is on that tumult of thoughts that crowd our mind, trying to interpret what we are seeing.

Without knowing it, inside we are always trying to find out the reason why certain events are happening around us, through a series of thoughts that are always moving from one side to another, occupying all our mental space, trying to understand reality, to understand those segments of information that are coming to us from outside, that we are capturing through our perception.

Our thoughts begin to reproduce one after the other, trying to grasp what is most important. Usually we do not pay attention to this activity that is taking place, because we remain attentive to other things that exist outside.

WHAT DIVIDES US

When we pay attention to certain mental contents, we can somehow be distancing ourselves from ourselves, from what we really are, and from what is important to achieve our true purpose.

This kind of thoughts that take us away from what we really are, we can distinguish them in our inner voice: in that inner speech that we can observe when we talk to ourselves in certain moments of the day.

It is there, in that instant, where all the contents that we have in our mind unfold: they are nothing more than the fruit of the mental structure that we have been creating over time, through a series of elements that come from our memory and that manage to gain a foothold in our consciousness, to the point that they have been absorbing us, leading us, marking the direction we should follow, while we have been abandoning ourselves, obeying without putting any impediment.

When we contemplate all this that happens inside; when we listen and observe that inner voice that tries to associate some thoughts with others, we will realize what it is that separates us, what divides us; the kind of thoughts that attract us most; the ones that trap us and take us over, stealing our calm and our tranquility when they rush uncontrollably over our consciousness, mixing with images of the past and going up and down along our mind in a mechanical way.

THEY DRIVE US

Thoughts are what direct us, that is why we must pay attention to everything that passes through our mind. All those contents influence us in what we do, because the elements that in every moment are in our mind impel us to carry out a series of actions that in many occasions we execute in an unconscious way, since we do not pay attention to those thoughts that join in our conscience and that are in the origin of our behaviors.

It is for this reason that we must be attentive to certain thoughts; since, if they remain for a long time in our mind, in the end they force us to execute a series of acts in a mechanical way, which may be repeated very often over time and become habits that are then difficult to eliminate.

We must bear in mind that all those thoughts that appear in our inner voice, can influence us in some way, because if they are very dominant they can lead us, drive us, and in the end we end up obeying them without thinking about the consequences that following a certain line of thought or some concrete ideas about a particular matter can bring us.

TOXIC THOUGHTS

It is we ourselves who decide to live in the dark. We accumulate anguish without knowing it, every time we allow a set of negative thoughts to settle in our mind that little by little take over our consciousness, in such a way that in the end they manage to penetrate our own judgments, our reasoning and all those interpretations that we make about those things that happen to us.

Sometimes we allow ourselves to be assaulted by negative contents, without realizing the consequences that this can bring us.

This way of thinking, which often takes hold of us, causes us uneasiness, suffering, but we hardly appreciate it. Only with the passage of time we become aware that there is something inside us that is accumulating, that is slowly hitting us and that is consuming us, exhausting us, declining us towards a restlessness that little by little begins to cultivate in our inner world.

Negative reflections

Reflections originate in my mind that once they begin, they never seem to end. Some of them lead me to disenchantment, because they are accompanied by limiting affirmations that obfuscate me, as they always insist on collecting the negative in me. They are attached to conflict, to everything that can oppress me at any given moment.

Sometimes these thoughts are chained together, and if they are negative, they create an internal conflict that leads you to suffering, to sadness, so that you slowly enter a distressing and cruel world, because of what is happening in your mind.

They have the faculty of accompanying me for long periods of time, because they are added, without me being very conscious of it, to all those ideas that are produced in my mind.

In those moments it is difficult for me to find harmony, something that links me with tranquility. I try to seek order, to reconcile myself with myself; but all that, which disturbs me so much mentally, vibrates so strongly within me that I always find it very difficult to regulate all that confusion.

Sometimes I need some time to organize my ideas: that constant narration that I have in my head about the things that happen to me, and that sometimes is not totally true; sometimes it is perverted by a whole series of explanations that follow one after the other and that deform reality. They are outlining a point of view in me totally wrong, inconsistent.

All that arises in my mind divides me; it distances me from what I really am. All that I have in my head makes me hesitate, waste energy, lose my temperance, which I only obtain when I find stillness, when I convince myself that I am not what I am thinking at that moment.

Sometimes my reason loses its common sense, it does not evaluate, it does not value properly. It does not solve complications; nor does it eliminate suffering; nor does it suppress sadness. It lets itself be carried away by events, without making decisions.

Sometimes my reason leads me away from the truth. It is not aware of the harm that some thoughts can do me, when they dissolve in my mind.

My understanding, at times, is imprecise, defective. It makes me see things always in the same way, without warning me when there is falsehood; when deception hovers over my ideas.

Many times my reason can lead me to misfortune, when it fills my conscience with negative manifestations, which allows itself to be influenced by that tangle of unconscious contents that sprout in my mind with the idea of distancing me from what I really am.

Back to being me

Therefore, I cannot allow my consciousness to be fattened with polluting elements, because they merge with each other until they manage to create a confusion in me that is then difficult to eradicate.

I cannot abandon myself to all that disorder created by my own thoughts. I feel that I must concentrate on conquering that space in my mind where my reflections begin and all those questions that I ask myself about everything that happens to me and about life in general.

I am more and more aware that I must not forget myself; that I must throw out of me everything that upsets me, everything that tries to bring me down; that is what I must worry about.

I know that if I get rid of all those harmful thoughts that try to harm me, I will be me again. I am aware that all those thoughts that spread throughout my mind have nothing to do with me, with who I really am.

Learning to distinguish them

In these cases it is advisable to make an effort to become aware of what is oppressing us. It is necessary that we consider the cause of that which is causing us restlessness, of that which is destroying our inner calm.

Then we will discover the source, the origin. We will approach the truth of what is happening to us; it is the best way to find an explanation to that restlessness that we experience in many moments. In this way we can calm our own agitation, we can clearly understand what is causing us distress.

If we get used to perform this exercise frequently, we will be able to attenuate the suffering caused by this mental activity in which negative thoughts are incorporated in an impulsive way; so that they are lodged in our consciousness to remain there as long as possible.

If we carry out this practice, we can anticipate, exercise an opposition to that mechanism of our own mind that in many occasions we are increasing it without knowing it, when we do not pay attention to all that that manifests in our conscience, in a repetitive and unconscious way.

We cannot allow all those contents that are not beneficial for us to spread in our own mind. We must know how to diminish them, to protect ourselves from this process that sometimes is activated without realizing it and begins to supply our mind with toxic thoughts, illusory ideas, which take over our judgments and our reason.

We must learn to distinguish them, it is the only way to clarify our mind, to return calm to our inner world.

It is possible if we persevere in a constant way, if we do not allow ourselves to be absorbed by that frenetic activity to which we are accustomed, which takes place without us being very conscious of it.

Through your inner voice you can know them more deeply, because that is where they manifest and become visible to capture your attention. That is where they show themselves, where they appear. It is only a matter of investigating a little, of examining yourself, through that inner speech that tries to impress you without you realizing it, so that in the end it ends up determining you, guiding you in an established direction.

If you find out the origin of this kind of thoughts that manifest themselves in that internal chatter that we all have, you will be able to build another more objective vision of reality. You will stop being driven by all those thoughts that try to mold you, to reduce you to a concrete idea, to limit you.

If we manage to stop them

If we manage to stop all these thoughts that incline us to leave the path that leads to our true purpose, then we will reach the mastery of our own mind.

If we manage to push them away, we feel a relief when we see that our mind begins to cleanse itself, to shake off all those toxic thoughts that only manage to fill us with contradictions when they spread through our consciousness.

Once we manage to expel all these contents, we will feel that optimism begins to spread; we begin to observe everything with different eyes, with a cleaner look, with a more lucid vision of the world, of the reality that surrounds us.

We will begin to value everything in a less destructive, less negative way, since we will have abandoned all those negative thoughts that try to destroy us when they are integrated in our mind.

We will feel an inner well-being that will rush through our whole body. This will cause a tranquility and calmness that will spread throughout that inner world that we all have inside.

If you manage to stop them, you will find a greater clarity in your reasoning, at the same time that all that confusion that corrodes you inside and that is installed inside you almost automatically will disappear.

If you manage to separate yourself from all that which causes you confusion, you will be able to divert your attention elsewhere. Then all that internal discord that has been deceiving you for so long will disappear and the only thing it produces is discomfort, affliction and an internal confusion that causes you a restlessness that makes you live in constant uncertainty.

Then you can get to the beginning, to the origin of all those toxic thoughts that have been building up inside you, causing damage to your state of mind, your willpower, even upsetting your own personality.

Without knowing it, many of these thoughts can envelop you without you understanding anything. You only let yourself be exalted by their strength, when they rise to your mind. They absorb you at the same time that they make you experience suffering, that you think in a certain way, that you come to believe what you are not in reality.

It depends on the focus

If we give importance to certain contents, they will end up affecting us, determining us; they will influence our state of mind, our emotions. We can feel happy or unhappy depending on the kind of thoughts we have.

If we allow negative contents about life and about ourselves to settle in our mind, this ends up affecting us; in such a way that we will have a negative vision of the world and of everything that surrounds us, even of the people we have around us.

We will see everything from a negative point of

view that will influence us in our way of facing difficulties, in order to solve the problems that arise in our daily life.

That is why we must be especially careful in what we think, in what we put our attention. We must stop for a while and reflect on whether what we keep in our mind will be positive or not in the future.

In reality, we are the consequence of what we think, of the interpretations we have made, of everything that has happened to us before.

Depending on where we put our focus, so will be our attitude towards certain things; so will be our way of behaving and being in the world. So our relationships will also be affected in some way, by all that we have in our mind at every moment, by all that passes through our consciousness.

THE SAME THOUGHTS

Sometimes we can't get an idea out of our head, and we always think about the same things a thousand times. Perhaps we give too much importance to a certain kind of contents that, in reality, do not lead us to anything.

We tend to turn frequently on the same thoughts, many of which do not lead to an end, to an objective that is profitable.

A characteristic of these thoughts is that they persist and are constantly repeated in our consciousness, so that they generate a series of difficulties that in the end we cannot control.

This kind of thoughts can accompany us for long periods of time, they can agitate us inside, until in the end they manage to combine with other similar ones and can wrap everything in an anguish from which in the end we cannot escape. They become so strong that we cannot change them.

The truth is that we spend too much energy focusing almost always on the same thoughts. What really matters goes unnoticed many times because of the accumulation of information that we have in our mind, and to which we pay too much attention, leaving aside what could really be beneficial.

You stay there, for long periods of time, around the same idea, the same thoughts. This is why it is important to observe oneself, because this happens within each one of us.

Establish control

If we have enough ability to realize that this happens, we can control ourselves in some way; we can prevent this mental mechanism from dominating us at each passing moment. We can put, in this way, a barrier, a dike of containment to all that set of automatic mental processes that overwhelm us suddenly, constantly.

For this it is important that we learn to be in silence and that we practice meditation; or the observation of ourselves, of our thoughts. It is the only way to reach the domain of our mind, of all that happens inside, that tries to control us and to direct us.

It is only a matter of putting a little will on our part and doing this exercise frequently. Only in this way we will see results, we will see that we can take control. It is a way to stop our thinking and to direct it in some way.

In this way we will end up thinking about what we really want and not what our mind proposes at any given moment.

If we act in this way, we will not let ourselves be carried away by the first thing that comes into our heads. We will learn to observe ourselves and to reflect before acting, to evaluate the different options before making a decision or choosing a path.

Establish changes

It can be difficult for us to stop thinking because we are not used to it. By our very nature we tend to be always scheming some idea in our mind; we tend to always focus on the same content. Even if we introduce new information, there are certain thoughts that always run through our head for certain periods of time, which are usually always the same and occupy our attention, preventing us from thinking about other things.

All this is because we give them great importance, for some reason they are significant for us and it is difficult for us to ignore them, to fix our gaze on other contents.

Only when we are aware of the consequences of fixating on certain ideas, of constantly repeating the same thoughts, we try to make a change. Then we consider that we should not pay too much attention to those elements and we start to consider the possibility of focusing on others.

This is how we function most of the time. Only when we are conscious, we try to establish some modification to try to avoid that which is damaging us, harming us in some way.

There are those who do not realize this and remain for long periods of time with the same thoughts, repeating themselves over and over again in their mind. They can even spend years with the same ideas in their head. They are incapable of making any change because they are not aware of this mechanism that reproduces itself over and over again, wasting energy that could be spent on other matters.

BEHAVIORS

Sometimes we let ourselves be guided by the first thing we think, we do not stop to reflect, even for a moment, on the consequences of each decision we make.

And all this is because we function unconsciously most of the time. We let ourselves be guided by every thought that arises in our mind, without considering the consequences.

A thought can lead us to a certain action if we pay too much attention to it. If it is repeated frequently, it will eventually result in a specific behavior, which we will execute because we have given relevance to that thought in our mind.

Depending on the importance we give to all those contents that arise in our consciousness, so will be our actions. Therefore, it is necessary that we consider the need to be more attentive to all that we think at a given moment, since it can direct us without us being very conscious of it.

Our behaviors, in some way, are conditioned by all

that which is previously presented in our mind; as it is exposed, it determines the path we should follow.

We could say that this is the beginning of our behaviors, which in some way determine our own personality. If our thoughts, or all those contents that arise in our mind, are confused, all our actions will also be confused. There will be no common thread, no balance, no coherence; and more importantly, there will be a division between what we do and what we really think we should do.

And all because we allow ourselves to be contaminated by that inner chatter, in such a way that we give it an importance it should not have.

Therefore, we must separate ourselves from its activity, from that current that has its origin in our own thoughts and that forms a world that we limit ourselves to accept without carrying out a previous analysis, or a conscious observation, of this whole system that orders us what we should do in each moment.

If we look at that voice that we all have in our heads, which are nothing more than our own repetitive thoughts, we will understand many of our behaviors. We will realize that many of them are related to that voice, with that mental content that is repeated insistently and that in the end leads us to a certain action.

Being attentive

At first, the influence of our own thoughts may seem insignificant, but over time, if they are associated with other similar thoughts and begin to repeat themselves constantly, they eventually end up driving our attention, taking over and directing even our own actions.

We must get used to be attentive to all those moments in which this occurs, since it is there when our mind begins to take control of our own will. This is the origin of our automatic behaviors, of our unconscious activity, which in many moments of the day we experience and extend over time.

Everything we do, in reality, is the fruit of what we continuously think. If we pay a little attention and are observant, we will realize the enormous influence that our thoughts and the other elements that appear in our consciousness have.

10. Living in fiction

We often live in a state of bewilderment because what we think distances us from reason. There are things that we do not understand very well; about which we do not get an answer, a meaning, but we continue to strengthen them in our mind, applying all kinds of thoughts about them, fabricating ideas and interpretations of the world that are hardly real.

Many of these thoughts can disguise reality, can make us believe in a non-existent world, force us to perceive things that do not really exist in the real world.

In this way we come to feed fantasies that, when we check them, we realize that they are not true, that we have allowed ourselves to be led by a deception that we have been supplying through unreal thoughts that have been covering reality with the mantle of our own imagination.

It can cause us to move away from the world in which we live, to experience a greater satisfaction in that other world only created in our own mind, where everything is possible and we do not find difficulties; as it happens in life itself, in the world that is out there, in the context that surrounds us and in which we usually live.

All this has its origin in our own mind. If we do not protect ourselves and do not realize what is happening there, in that space, it is easy for us to let ourselves be manipulated by our own thoughts, or by all those unconscious impulses that arise mechanically and incite us to act in an uncontrolled way on some occasions.

IMAGINATION

If we pay enough attention, we will realize that many contents that arise through this mechanism are false. They are not elements on which we have reflected, because we hardly have enough time to stop and analyze them.

They are compressed there, in our consciousness, through an unconscious process of our own mind. We cannot put them off or eliminate them if we are not aware of them. When we are, we can clearly observe how they are created, what their origin is, and how we get used to them and accept them without further ado.

We build imaginary ideas and beliefs that only exist in our own imagination, and all because we allow ourselves to be snatched by all those mental representations that we magnify in our conscience, in such a way that they become bigger and bigger and in the end they become thoughts that are articulated with each other and that little by little take us to another reality, to a parallel and closed world that has nothing to do with the one that exists outside, in our immediate environment.

Many times we are the ones who strengthen this unreal world, because it is less annoying, or because we do not find the frustration that we experience in the one we usually live in.

That is why we end up living in a fantasy, in a false illusion that we strengthen over time, covering it with new contents, with new thoughts to which we get used to without realizing the deception that we are creating about ourselves.

We allow ourselves to be contaminated

If we immerse ourselves in that voice that we all have in our head, it is possible that we allow ourselves to be contaminated by all those mental representations that are more typical of the imagination than of reality. We will live in a world close to fiction, composed of impossible illusions that we will mature little by little, within a sea of contradictions that will end up imposing themselves.

Sometimes things may happen to you that you do not know how to define them very well, that the diversity of events to which you are exposed is so diverse that it is difficult for you to find a harmony to establish a certain distance and place everything in its place.

We do not always have enough time to observe ourselves and thus free ourselves from everything that is hindering our own happiness. Many times we live in a permanent indecision that we do not know how to moderate.

Frustration

Many times we are astonished when we discover that this fiction, invented by ourselves, has nothing to do with reality; when we realize that our imagination has played a trick on us.

Then we are aware of the time we have spent feeding false illusions, so inconsistent that they were a deception to ourselves.

This is what often leads us to that feeling of frustration that little by little punishes us, creating a great division in our inner world.

When we prevent it

When we have the opportunity to prevent our own imagination from taking over us, we stop inventing all those false and contradictory realities that we often create without realizing it, when we pay attention in a thoughtless way to a series of thoughts that have no reason to be.

In this way we come to understand ourselves much better, because the truth is always connected with what we really are. When we identify ourselves with thoughts, we move away from our true self, from our true nature.

OUR OWN VISION

We must pay attention to all that is constantly being added to our mind, because there are elements that are being joined with other similar ones and are shaping our vision of reality.

All this is what makes us inclined to see life in a certain way. In truth, our point of view on everything we observe is based on the mental structure that we have built up over time.

With each experience we have learned a new lesson

that we have added to our memory. When this new knowledge emerges in our mind, it shapes a specific way of thinking that makes us see reality in a specific way.

This way of thinking determines our way of perceiving the world and everything that happens in it. If we examine ourselves a little, we will become aware of our way of thinking. We can detect, in many of our statements, if we are making a mistake, if we are moving away from the truth.

We can grasp it clearly when we observe the thought, when we direct our gaze to that inner voice that constantly repeats to us in a mechanical way all that we think at every moment.

All this then leaves an imprint in our memory, which will shape our knowledge of things, which in reality are contents that we convert, that we interpret from our own subjective point of view.

The conclusions we reach may resemble the truth, or they may remain distant. The fact is that, in the end, we get used to our own vision of things, without being very aware that we may be living in a permanent deception.

Contents that come together

Our own mental structures are nothing more than sets of contents that are joined with other similar thoughts, in such a way that they end up taking hold of us, providing us with a vision of the concrete reality; which can be true or not, depending on the objectivity of our perception, on our vision of the world and on how our previous experiences have been, on the results we have obtained through our own actions.

All the information we have accumulated will be related to all these factors, so that in the end it will show us a reality that may be similar to the one that exists outside, but it may also happen that this personalized vision of the world is very far from what really happens.

We can only verify this with the passage of time, with the result of our own actions and with the information that comes to us in our relationship with others; everything that others tell us about their own experiences.

Until we finally create our own peculiar vision of things. This is what drives us to continue surviving, because the information we obtain helps us to solve the different difficulties that arise along our path.

Wrong vision

Many of these contents may be wrong, they may contain an erroneous vision of life, of the world around us, of the people around us.

It may be that many of these memories that are stored in our memory were not properly analyzed at the time.

That is why there are many contents that we assimilated at the time that can later lead us to confusion, as they are irrational. And it is that, in many occasions, when we have some experience, we do not take time to reflect on what has happened to us, in such a way that in the end we end up having erroneous interpretations of reality.

We can end up having a wrong vision of the events

that we once had the opportunity to live. All of this is stored in our memory and can later arise again, altering our vision of things.

It depends on the information

The more information we obtain, the more possibilities we will have when it comes to solving those problems that arise.

People who have hardly any contact with reality, with the world around them, have more difficulties in finding solutions to their own problems, due to lack of contact with the outside world. As a consequence they have a lack of the information that is required to find a way out of all those difficulties that one is having over time.

That is why it is important to have a good relationship with the people around us, because from there we can obtain information that can help us to face our problems; we will have more options if we act in this way.

BE AWARE

All this is stored in our own mind. If we do not observe it, we can remain submerged in a constant storm without being aware of it.

If we are not aware of this and we do not separate ourselves from this kind of contents, they become permanent and take over our own reasoning and build an irrational world composed of a whole amalgam of uncertain beliefs, which are deposited in our memory after so much repetition, they join one with another in such a way that they sow confusion in our consciousness.

Therefore, we must be aware of all those thoughts that try to lead us, that are constantly articulated in our consciousness without a determined direction.

It is important to be aware that there are a series of thoughts that can transform the reality we observe into something very different from what it really is, so that we can deceive ourselves when interpreting the events that happen to us and the circumstances in which we live.

Being conscious helps us in some way to free all those elements, all that disorder that makes us live in confusion, in disorder. We will manage to suppress all those irrational thoughts that make us interpret reality in a wrong way, that are integrated in our conscience without a previous analysis on our part.

NOT TO BE INDIFFERENT

We cannot let ourselves be carried away by our own alterations. We must have a certain discipline not to neglect ourselves, not to let ourselves be impressed by some confusing thoughts that are repeated in a permanent way. We cannot allow our energy to be wasted on obscure and insignificant thoughts.

We cannot be obstinate in following always in the same direction, when it does not really lead anywhere. We have to know, first, where we are going, what we are looking for, why we are determined to continue on a particular path.

We have to know how to orient all these elements that are in our inner world. I believe this is the best solution to our problems. If we allow ourselves to be subjected to the constant deception of our mind, our suffering will increase until we lose our peace of mind.

If we remain indifferent to this inner dialogue, unwanted thoughts will accumulate in our mind; they will actively move through our consciousness giving an unreal meaning to everything we perceive.

We have to learn to separate what is a mere figment of our imagination from reality itself.

BE ATTENTIVE

When we perceive what is outside of us, we have to pay special attention to every detail of everything that is in front of us.

If we are careless and do not pay attention, we will not grasp the essence of things. We will let ourselves be impressed by appearances, we will not keep the relevant information, the one that really matters.

For this it is necessary that we are attentive to all those components that arise in our mind. If we allow ourselves to be seduced, we will allow ourselves to be deceived and we will not be able to distinguish reality very well.

If we want to improve ourselves, we must pay attention to our judgments, the way we associate our thoughts and the way we reason.

On many occasions we accept irrational beliefs as if they were true, we group together ideas that make no sense and we become familiar with them. We get used to this way of thinking without realizing that it can influence our future, our destiny.

Our gaze, therefore, must be attentive, but not conditioned by the mind, by the past. We must allow everything to flow around us, not intervening, letting things happen by themselves; not manipulating reality to our liking, not trying to distort things to suit our way of thinking. We must perceive reality as it is, without the need to make changes to transform it into something else.

Everything that happens around us has a reason for being, so we must remain attentive to know the causes behind everything that happens around us. If we know how to make a correct reading in each moment, we will find the best decisions and solutions to each of the difficulties that we are facing.

On the other hand, if our interpretation of the facts is not sufficiently objective, we will not know how to find the solution to our problems, we will keep them in time without having the opportunity to find a way out.

When we perceive the world, we must do it with a clean, clear look, free from the conditioning of the mind. This is the only way to have a clear vision of things, of events and of all the experiences we have lived throughout our lives.

We cannot allow that the memories and all those conditionings of the past make us believe in a reality that does not exist, or that force us to interpret the world in a wrong way, far from what is really happening.

11. Reality

Sometimes, our thoughts propose us an interpretation that has nothing to do with the truth, with what is really happening, and we approve it without further ado. We are not aware in those moments that this can generate confusion, since we are accepting a vision of the world that is very different from the one that really exists.

We do not realize that we may be transforming reality, giving it a meaning different from the real one, trying to channel the facts that we are observing by another path, directing them towards another reality very different from the one that is.

Our mind has this peculiar way of acting. Many times it deforms the events leaving aside what really matters of what is happening. It begins to relate some thoughts with others, until in the end it ends up building a very subjective vision of the world.

We let ourselves be easily convinced by our own mind, by all those judgments that are freely created and that can be clearly observed in that internal dialogue that we have, through our own inner voice that is where thoughts and all that mental activity that takes place when we stop to examine a particular point of the world around us to try to reach the understanding of what we are seeing.

INTERPRETATION

Our mind is vast, immense, although there are only the representations to which we pay attention. Those are the ones that in the end gain strength, in all that vast world that is our consciousness.

When we are indifferent to what happens there and do not reflect, our own thoughts impose themselves on us. In such a way that we allow ourselves to be contaminated by all those ideas that are projected into our consciousness, creating a false interpretation of reality, an inaccurate vision of things -which spreads throughout our mind- that ends up creating an illusion, a mistaken vision of the world, different from the one that is presented outside on a daily basis.

And all this is done under our consent, without us having the mastery of all these processes that try to coordinate themselves in our own consciousness, without us being very conscious of it.

False vision

Everything has a meaning. Sometimes we can deduce it, but at other times we don't get it right with the explanations we give ourselves. We rush to draw conclusions very quickly and in the end they are nothing more than interpretations that we make of our own reality.

What we think may not be what is happening, perhaps it belongs more to the desire for it to be so.

Many times we fail to evaluate accurately what is

happening in the external world. We allow ourselves to be carried away by appearances and many other influences that cause us not to see the truth. For that reason many of our thoughts are not correct; they are accompanied by a false vision of the world, of the facts that happen to us, and this determines that in many cases we deceive ourselves mixing some things with others, creating a confusion in our way of seeing the reality that is moving us away from what it really is.

This is why sometimes we have an altered vision of things, creating false interpretations of everything that happens around us. This is the reason why we devise misleading beliefs that take hold of us and set us in a certain direction.

In truth, everything depends on how we interpret what happens to us, on how we organize the information. If this information is confusing and does not adjust to reality, we will encounter difficulties or problems that we will not know how to solve.

Conjectures

Some of our conclusions can become conjectures that only exist in our own imagination, that accumulate there and that fill our mind with a series of beliefs that later we continue thinking that they are true, so that we can develop a false world, through all those unconscious interpretations that in many occasions we set in motion, when we dare to make a judgment of what is happening to us.

Once all these ideas are installed in our mind, we cannot give them up so easily. They do not cease to cease, to swing along our consciousness, so that we get used to them and we act according to these contents, to the direction that these thoughts are leading us.

It leads us to confusion

That is why many of those judgments that rush into our consciousness are not the most sensible, and that is why our reason does not act in a logical way. There are many confusing thoughts that are mixed with each other and in the end they create a restlessness to which we get used to.

We think that this is normal. Most of the time we do not find the calm that we need, because through our mind a series of elements spread out, joining one with the other, producing a torment and an affliction that erases our tranquility and our joy.

Our way of interpreting the world can lead us to anguish, if we do not know how to analyze correctly all those manifestations that we observe outside.

If in our internal conversation we sow negative thoughts, we will end up having a negative vision of reality, so that many of our interpretations of what happens to us will also be negative.

Therefore, we often make mistakes in our own actions, and we do not recognize ourselves when we end up doing something that does not correspond to who we really are.

UNDERSTANDING REALITY

We create a world different from the real one, because we limit ourselves to follow the subjective conclusions that we build, which are concentrated in our memory and then manifest themselves again to try to confirm them.

We cannot resign ourselves to believe everything we think. We have to be aware that many of these thoughts arise without our consent and that they separate us from reality, from what is happening outside, in the external world.

Therefore, we must be attentive to our conversation, to that internal chatter where we talk to ourselves, trying to examine and recognize what we have in front of us, because that is where many confusions and many errors are generated in the interpretation of the world that exists around us.

It is there where we elaborate many theories about what we see that in some cases are wrong, or are limited to take into account only a part of reality, leaving aside other aspects that must also be taken into account.

Perhaps, the secret of true knowledge lies there, in that moment in which we draw our own conclusions from the experiences we have. Depending on how we gather that kind of information, our vision of things, of the reality that surrounds us, of life, of the world we live in will be the same.

If our final conclusions are wrong, this will affect our way of reasoning, our judgments, which will come together to form beliefs that in the end we will follow and that will come to dominate us; and that will then be transferred to that inner dialogue that we all have with ourselves; that is marking us the direction to follow in a discreet way, without us being very aware of it.

We must be attentive to all this exchange of information that takes place in our own mind in certain situations, because it is the moment when we try to understand what is happening.

If our way of understanding reality is wrong, imperfect, this will create difficulties for us to find the truth, to try to repair what is wrong, what we have made a mistake.

In this way we will not be able to find solutions to the different difficulties that life presents us. All that information that we perceive and that we assimilate, in the end we end up contaminating it, distancing it from the truth.

The origin of everything

The origin of everything is in the way we interpret reality: what happens to us at any given moment. If we select well our judgments and our reasoning, we will think sensibly, we will arrive at logical statements about what we are seeing; and this will be beneficial for us, since later, when we find ourselves in a similar situation, all those conclusions that we once drew about that matter will arise again. If the information we obtained at the time was adequate, this will be beneficial, since it will help us to be objective, to understand perfectly what is happening at that moment. It will not be necessary for us to look for an explanation to try to clarify ourselves. It will not be necessary for us to examine in detail what is happening in order to understand it.

In our interpretation of reality is the foundation of our vision of the world, of life, and of how we see ourselves. In that inner voice that we all have, we can observe how all those thoughts that arise in our mind in relation to what we are living in each moment are manifested. We can see what kind of thoughts they are, if they are helping us to understand reality or if they are leading us to a confusion that has no way back.

OBJECTIVE REALITY

For this we must remain attentive to those thoughts that arise in our mind when we are facing a given situation. We have to perceive clearly what it is that arises in our mind in those moments, because that content is what will lead us to value that concrete reality that occurs at that moment in a certain way.

Surely, in those moments in our mind, many related contents that we have stored in our memory will arise. All these elements will try to unite with each other to elaborate a judgment, a reasoning that makes us understand the situation we have in front of us.

We have to be aware in those moments that we can be wrong in the type of assessment we make. We are not always right, we are not sufficiently objective, because in certain occasions our judgments are not the correct ones and are far away from the truth, from what it really is.

Just because we have thought it does not mean that it is true, we can make mistakes in the type of approach we make when assessing reality. That is why we should not trust what is produced in our own mind, since we may be deceiving ourselves without being very aware of it.

That is why it is important to observe things as objectively as possible, far from the judgments of the mind and all those thoughts that may arise in those moments and that have some relation with what we have in front of us.

When everything is observed from that inner look that we have and that many do not know, reality is seen in an objective way; if one perceives things without judging them, without putting labels, without previous prejudices. This requires a knowledge of our inner workings.

OBSERVE

If we pause and observe all that movement of thoughts, we can penetrate into our way of reflecting, of analyzing reality. We can see if it is defective, if we can improve it.

It is only a matter of investigating a little in that inner voice that we all have, where we can glimpse all those thoughts that assail us at a given moment and that have to do with what we are living in each situation.

If we manage to place ourselves in this situation of observation, we can somehow moderate everything that we appreciate in our conscience, everything that is causing us some damage.

Benefits

This is one of the great benefits that we obtain if we observe ourselves, if we intervene on our own mental processes. All this will give rise to a new consciousness, to a new vision of the world, to another way of interpreting reality more in accordance with the truth, with what each thing is.

We will not have the need to create a parallel world, to invent a new reality to hide the existing one, because we will have enough tools to adapt to each of the circumstances we live, since our vision will be much more objective, much closer to the truth.

Each and every one of the decisions we make will be much more effective in resolving the various difficulties that we go through throughout life. All this will make us have a new attitude towards things. We will not have the need to run away from problems, from reality, from difficulties; nor will we allow our mind to elaborate a parallel world through our own imagination, which leads us to an evasion or to directly deny the reality of things.

Therefore, in the future, we will not feel so much frustration when things do not go as we intend, because we will be prepared to observe them with a clarity that will help us to overcome the obstacles that arise at every step we take.

ANALYZE

Everything comes from the same place. That is why it is important that we get our thoughts right, in our way of analyzing the things we see, in what happens to us, in the way we interpret life and everything that the people around us tell us.

Then everything will be more sensible. We will not live in that violent confusion that shakes us inside and that influences all those decisions that we take daily and that is marking the course and our own destiny.

Our way of thinking is what gives us the clarity we

need to understand reality and to understand ourselves. We only have to notice how our thoughts act
when analyzing each experience we have. If we are attentive we can see the path they follow, if there is coherence in the conclusions we are drawing; if there is
an order in the information we are using; if the sources
are reliable or if we are getting carried away by the
appearances of things.

It is a matter of discovering what is behind everything that emerges. We cannot exclude any detail, because everything that exists around us creates the reality
we see.

12. Inner space

Within us there is a secret: there is a space where all difficulties disappear, where problems cease to be exposed and you do not feel contaminated by the deception of your own thoughts.

It is like a deep space, beyond our own thoughts, which cannot be explained.

It is just a matter of appreciating it. When one penetrates within oneself, through reflection and meditation, and immerses oneself in one's inner world, it is when one can conquer and take hold of that other deep dimension where one experiences another kind of more conscious observation.

In those moments one directs one's gaze towards oneself and distances oneself from all those imaginary elements that constantly circulate in our mind, which burden our own consciousness until they create an uneasiness that mortifies us little by little.

ANOTHER LEVEL OF CONSCIOUSNESS

Sometimes I feel present, especially when I am concentrated in my inner world and I do not let myself be driven by the pressure of my own thoughts, which penetrate my consciousness, always trying to find explanations for everything that happens.

I feel that I am reconciled with myself when I verify, through calmness, that there exists within me a space where all those mental contents that crowd my mind stop piling up.

When I am transported to that place, all my problems, most of them fictitious, are destroyed. I understand in those moments that I am in another level of consciousness, where I have the possibility of observing myself and everything that arises in my consciousness.

From there I can contemplate everything with another look, I do not let myself be surprised by the enchantment of the mind, nor do I let myself be confused by the force of the imagination. It is a place where I feel safe, where my creativity increases and I feel that I have control of myself.

I go to this place when I feel disoriented, when I feel that confusion and disorder take over me; it is a way to regain control of who I am.

This inner space is like my fortress, a means of defense against the abyss of my own mind, which through my thoughts forces me to travel through a world that bears no relation to what I really am.

If you can access it, you can recognize it in detail. It is another level of consciousness, something higher. It is above your own thoughts. You just need to find calm and observe yourself.

You will realize how you function inside; how you can communicate with yourself; how you can access that space separate from mental activity where any disturbance disappears and you are not carried away by your own emotions.

You will be aware that it is not so far away, that it can be reached if you let yourself be abandoned in silence and do not attend to all those memories stored in your memory.

In this situation we discover that there is an inner silence that freezes all that mental noise to which we are accustomed. We reach a stillness that takes us away from mental activity and begins to spread throughout our body. If we allow ourselves to be led by it, we will be at a higher level of consciousness, closer to spirituality, where we will feel free of all those mental representations that are repeated in our consciousness.

When we elevate ourselves to this other level of consciousness, contradictions and inconveniences disappear. Nothing stuns or distracts us.

If we have the ability to reach it, we will find ourselves in a situation in which we will feel a tranquility, an inner peace that will lead us to the true knowledge of things, of what we are; as if the darkness disappears from us and we are more conscious.

Creativity

When we reach this other point, which is consciousness without thought, we find ourselves with a huge empty space that is conducive to enhance our creativity, because we are not subject to all that stream of content that emanates repetitively from our mind.

Control

Only in this section, in this other dimension, we manage to take control of our own thoughts, to the extent that we are fully aware of everything we are observing. In such a way that we are the ones who can decide, at that moment, to which content to direct our attention, which element is important and which is not. At that moment we have total control of what is happening in our inner world.

We will have the opportunity to join those thoughts that are related, but in a controlled way, not unconsciously. This can enhance our own creativity, and can give rise to a new mental structure different from the one we build daily based on all those unconscious thoughts that arise in our mind.

ANOTHER DIMENSION

In reality, we all function on the basis of a program that we create in an unconscious way, by repeating a series of contents over and over again. If we detach ourselves from this mechanism, being aware that it exists, peace returns to us and we can use our focus of attention to place it in another place further away from all those elements that exist in our mind.

In this way we can have access to that other world that is also there, a little further away, where there is no thought that tries to dominate us, because in that space we only find a silence and emptiness that makes us not to rush, to find the calm and tranquility enough to find ourselves, away from the fog of the mind.

Only if we establish a pause in front of all that mental movement, we can access that other dimension where we can observe everything that happens in our inner world.

And we must be aware that, within us, there is also

an emptiness, a silence, within a dimension that is beyond the noise of our own mind.

There is a space that is free of mental contents. It is a part of our consciousness that is not occupied by thoughts, that is in that dimension where there is only silence and there is no external or internal influence of any kind.

It is also part of who we are, but we can only access it if we transcend all those contents that are in the form of thoughts.

If you manage to make everything stop, you will be aware that you enter another world, a spiritual and pure space far from the appearance of the mind.

To enter into contact with this other dimension is an experience that only occurs when you detach yourself from all influences.

AN ENCOUNTER WITH WHAT YOU ARE

I always try to stay awake, although it is not so easy. It is essential to try not to think too much; in this way you conquer a space within your consciousness that is freed from the noise of thoughts.

When you manage to place yourself there, you feel liberated in some way; it is as if you feel free of all those confusions that overwhelm you daily. At that moment something resplendent arises within you: suddenly you begin to feel a pleasant peace that slowly takes you away from the din of external stimuli, and also from all that impulsive mental activity to which you are accustomed.

You begin to feel less movement in your mind, as if many of the contents that live there begin to be extinguished. Then you forget everything and a silence that runs through all your arteries reminds you that you are in an uninhabited place, far from disorder and suffering.

When you conquer that place, you feel a different energy that makes everything slow down, and you experience a precise stillness that only originates in that deep state.

When you gain mastery of that inner space, there is an encounter with who you are. You can observe everything in a crystalline way; all your fears disappear and you stop perceiving that need to be constantly resorting to the past, which causes a great imbalance in you.

All this makes you reconcile with yourself, you leave aside the appearance, which has its origin in the false self: in the "ego", which is created in the mind through your own thoughts.

YOU FIND CLARITY

When we are able to reach this other dimension that exists within ourselves, we manage to have a much clearer vision of life, of what we are, of reality itself; as if we found the reason and we moved away from all those false beliefs that often contaminate us and keep us away from the truth of things.

In this state we see everything cleaner: with greater clarity. We do not see the obstacles that exist, nor all those negative impressions that often arise in our mind and that in most cases are absurd and irrational.

In this way, we will be able to get out of the prison of the mind, of the thoughts that separate us from what we are, from our true purpose. Only in this way we will find light, clarity; we will free ourselves from the bonds of the mind, from all those blockages to which we are sometimes subjected, that make us live in a permanent disorder, in a suffering that is expressed through all those thoughts that appear in our inner voice and that are displayed and repeated constantly placing us in another reality: the one we create in our own consciousness and that in many occasions is a dark reality, deceptive, separated from the world that surrounds us.

YOU FIND HARMONY

You do not feel the need to judge anything, you just need to be there, just to observe that place that you have conquered through your own calm and the control you have achieved over your own mind.

In that space you can find harmony, because nothing hinders you, everything is smoothed out. You come to discover your true nature; you reach the origin from which everything starts, getting to know in detail everything that separates you from what you really are.

You enter a state of vigilance where you feel that you are present, coexisting with a silence and stillness that seduce you and make you prudent.

You experience a stillness that gradually strengthens you. If you manage to maintain it over time, nothing will disturb you. You will feel that everything has an order within you and calmness will always accompany you. You will be reconciled with yourself and you will find harmony in all that great inner universe, where there are moments in which you let yourself be carried away by your own imagination.

UNION WITH YOURSELF

I feel that from there I can transform myself. It is like a meditation space that places me in the beginning, where everything originates. So I become aware of everything that separates me from myself, from what I really am.

When you gain control of that place, you come to feel a union with yourself; it is as if you establish a means of communication with another part of you that has always been hidden, but that you have not been able to discover because of all the mental obstacles that prevent you from having a clear and precise perception of all that is hidden within you.

It is where your true self is housed, that which you really are. It is in the very center of your inner self, which is where your true nature is.

Therefore, nothing can determine you if you just observe the course of what happens there. It is a good place to start building a new being, because nothing is contaminated there.

When you immerse yourself in your inner space, you feel that you are in control and that you are closer to wisdom, to true knowledge; at the same time a calmness spreads throughout your being.

When you can clearly distinguish that space, you become aware of your full potential. You acquire a knowledge of yourself that leads you to a full understanding of reality.

When you try to look beyond what you see, you experience a union with yourself that makes you feel that you are present, that you are really aware of everything that is happening. You feel a liberation that leads you to mastery of yourself, as you move away from all those constant disturbances to which you are habitually subjected.

This state leads you to understand all this internal mechanism, to know its components, to consider what makes you think in a certain way, which then ends up influencing your own decisions.

When we move away from the influences of the mind, we find greater security, because we are not invaded by all those annoying doubts that often hit us and make us change direction. From here it is possible to return to the right path, the path we must follow to reach our true purpose.

TO PUT REALITY IN ORDER

When I get everything to stop, the noise in my mind ends. All that abundance of thoughts ends and, therefore, so does the disorder and confusion. It is as if I change the direction of the main thread and my mind takes another direction.

Only from there you can have a wide vision of things; you can order reality in a different way, in a more objective way; you can separate the true from the false with ease; you can solve any difficulty, because you are more lucid to realize what causes confusion. Your reason is clothed in a logic that helps you to discover the truth, to understand that which was not clear to you, which was not understandable to you.

When you reach it, you reach true understanding. You will realize what destroys you, because there you will find the truth, in that serene and calm space where nothing can disturb you and where the order of all things is established.

In that place there is no chaos or disorder, you feel that everything is united in a proportional harmony that remains stable, while your attention remains there, in that space where everything begins.

When you extend yourself to this deeper level, you come to the mastery of everything that moves within your inner world. You observe all the manifestations that move through your consciousness, that slide along your mind trying to influence you, flooding your judgments and even your own reasoning with contents that have been accumulating in your memory and that you quickly recognize because they are habitual.

If you try to stay there, without intervening, then there will be no division in you. The thoughts in your mind will be like a faint whisper that will slowly fade away if you stand aside as if you were a mere observer, a simple witness.

Then tranquility will return to you, you will be fortunate because all the agitation of your mind will disappear. You will feel a pleasant, sudden sensation when your mind quiets down. You will be inclined to repeat this sensation on more occasions. At that moment you will be aware of what this discovery can mean. You will understand that it can be the beginning of a personal transformation that you can take advantage of to heal all those wounds of the past that have always remained there, in the depths of your memories.

You will quickly understand that it can be a turning point, an effective way to establish the inner order that you have been losing little by little over time, because of all the disturbances that have been taking hold of you in an impetuous way, because of which you have been imprisoned, many times, in a world that has been narrowing inside you.

YOU FREE YOURSELF FROM DECEPTION

When I access that inner space and rise above my own thoughts, I feel that I am free from the deception of my own mind and a calmness begins to flow in me that gradually settles throughout my body and causes me a lucidity that makes me have a vision of things very close to the truth.

In those moments I experience true balance, I control my anger, and I verify that my reasoning is no longer contradictory nor does it feed false beliefs.

In those moments I verify that I can discern in a different way, that my arguments are no longer contaminated by the false illusions of the imagination or by all those toxic contents that often manifest in my mind with the idea of transferring me to another reality very different from the one that really is.

All this is possible only when we reach that spiritual dimension within us, which makes everything stop, makes us indifferent to the memories of the past and forget all those repetitive thoughts that constantly consume us through an inner voice that remains there almost every hour of the day.

If we do not let ourselves be confused by it, we can observe what is hidden beyond, in that space where time does not exist, where you meet yourself and you can transform yourself, because there lies the origin of what you are: your true nature. Everything starts from there, from that pure place, far from the darkness of the mind.

YOU FREE YOURSELF FROM SUFFERING

If you stay in that spiritual dimension, which is within you, you will find serenity and free yourself from the suffering condensed in the thousands of thoughts that arise in your mind and that you then keep in your consciousness when you pay attention to them.

In this more spiritual dimension, the impressions of the past will cease to exist. There are no memories that can harm you with their emotional charge.

In those moments you keep yourself away from any influence of the material world, and also from that which manifests in your own mind in those moments. Nothing can obfuscate or alter you.

In this other dimension we do not find the limitations that many times we create ourselves, when it comes to realize some purpose. It is as if we were freeing ourselves from the slavery to which we are subjected, from all those limitations that our own mind imposes on us.

In that stillness, in that calmness, we do not suffer any kind of suffering, so it is the best place to transform ourselves.

Then you perceive that all the conflicts disappear, as if all the difficulties had been resolved. That there is no longer that constant worry about time: about what happened in the past and about everything that needs to be done in the future.

You feel that you are in an unshakable place, where

your usual thoughts cease to flourish and everything is clothed in a complete peace, impervious to the clatter of the mind and the meaning of time. You understand that it is a place where there are no memories -those impressions of your memory that come to dominate you when they are very intense-, and that it can be an appropriate refuge to find yourself, to contact your true essence: with what you really are, in the depths of yourself.

HIDDEN INFORMATION

I have always been interested in everything that remains hidden. You only have to look at many expressions of those who surround you regularly to see that there are gestures that give them away.

When we communicate with others, we do not provide all the information, we always keep something to ourselves, simply because we do not want it to be known, at least at those moments.

The reasons may be varied, but it happens very often that in those moments we do not usually have enough skill to make this go unnoticed.

If we are being observed, this can be clearly perceived by others in any small gesture we make that indicates some kind of doubt or hesitation.

There are people who can easily decipher the verbal language of others, as they are very observant and quickly pick up on any hint of falsehood or, in these cases, those unexpected inhibitions that clearly indicate that something is being hidden and that the other person is not providing all the information.

Some people convey their moods very easily. If you

are observant, you can easily notice what the other person may be feeling inside, when he/she is expressing him/herself or trying to communicate.

In the same way, we also find many people who are inexpressive, so that we have to be very attentive to everything they say to be able to extract some information about them, about their way of being or about what they may be feeling at that moment.

In any case, I think it is always positive to know how to read and detect in time the emotions of others. This has to do with the degree of empathy that each person has. It is clear that those who have a greater ability to appreciate everything that is behind every gesture, every look, get more information and therefore a greater knowledge of those around them.

This kind of wisdom is necessary when it comes to relationships, and also to gain an understanding of the causes behind the behavior of oneself and others.

In reality, our way of acting and being in front of others are nothing more than expressions of what we carry inside, they are nothing more than external manifestations of our own inner world, of everything that extends throughout the length and breadth of our own mind.

LOOKING BEYOND

It is only a matter of looking a little beyond what happens in our own consciousness, of knowing how to transcend it. Then we will be able to clarify many enigmas that have always remained there, located in our own memories, and many of our problems, which have their origin in our mind, will come to an end.

It is advisable to make a small effort to go beyond, because only there we can find ourselves; we can get away from the deception of our thoughts, from all that information that is accumulated in our memory and that through the mental mechanism tries to lead us, determining what we should do at every moment. So that, sometimes, we come to behave in an unconscious way, as if we were a robot, guided by our own mental programming: a programming that we have been developing over time, based on repetitions of behaviors.

A deeper level

Many times I discover that what really matters is not seen, that it is kept hidden, guarded. It is only accessible to those who know how to look beyond, to those who are accustomed to observe the hidden signals behind every gesture, every word, everything we do...

There are those who do not limit themselves only to perceive what is around them, they also have the ability to explore at a deeper level. They do not work as mechanically and unconsciously as the majority of people, because they observe the disorder and confusion in others without them noticing it.

They are people who know how to read the behavior of others very well. They perceive very quickly if people are happy or not, with just a glance; or if there is fear in them, or if they are living a life full of unpleasant setbacks.

All this they can guess very easily. They are not deceived by appearances; they have a complete vision of the personality of those who surround them, and very few times they are mistaken in their appreciations.

There are people who have learned to interpret reality quite objectively. They do not allow themselves to be fascinated by the deception of appearances, nor do they allow themselves to be transported by the spell of their own imagination to other fictitious, occasional worlds. They are people who are close to the truth, almost always. They are not chained to a single way of thinking and are suspicious of those who are always trying to convince others.

It is no accident that they have a great knowledge of what they are. All that wisdom, which resides deep within oneself, is manifested in the way they conduct themselves through life, in the way they solve their problems and in the way they relate to others.

They are usually quite balanced people, who treasure a great knowledge of what they are, who do not live in unconsciousness -like the rest-, who always pay close attention to what is around them, to what others communicate, because there they integrate all the elements they need to obtain the information.

Therefore, they are aware of every detail, they know how to locate the causes of each incident and they are not indifferent to all the stimuli around them. They are aware that many of them can alter their calm, incite them to change course, to take a different path.

They are people who know how to rectify in time. They do not allow all those toxic thoughts that often lead us to observe reality in an inaccurate way.

A deeper look

I have always been interested in that spiritual dimension that we all carry inside. Throughout my experience I have been able to see how some people have been transformed thanks to the observation of that which apparently remains hidden but has always been there, in the deepest part of ourselves.

They have been able to do so because they have understood the mechanism, thanks to the attention they have paid when they have looked at themselves and discovered the origin, when they have found the way to go beyond, to transcend their own thoughts and contact that space where their own essence is, where one can find that spiritual dimension where one can reach clarity and come to the knowledge of their true nature.

It can be seen at a glance that this kind of people are more spiritual, because they observe everything with a much deeper look. They are conscious at all times of their own actions. They live in the present without thinking about the past; with a temperance and a calmness in everything they do, they walk through life lightly.

It is clear that they do not live in another reality, that they do not feel the need to invent other worlds to forget about this one. Their actions are limited to the present, without being determined by what may happen later, in the future.

Their endeavor is to discover all that is within their inner world. Their greatest aspiration is to know themselves, to observe all those manifestations that are inside, trying to reproduce all those contents that are in their memory.

For this kind of person it is essential not to deviate from that space, from that center where the encounter with what they really are takes place. They understand that only in that interval can the truth be observed.

GO TO THE ORIGIN

If we place ourselves at the beginning, where everything begins, we will find the meaning of all those things that have happened to us. The setbacks, the adversities, the misfortunes, everything obeys to a cause that is in the origin.

If we investigate within ourselves, we can discover it; if we know how to go to the beginning, to the birth, where we began to build a structure of contents through a series of thoughts that our own mental mechanism was suggesting us at the time.

If we want to clean our mind, we must do this. If we want to avoid and end our suffering, we must perform this exercise of observation of ourselves. Then we will be able to go to the beginning, where a way of thinking was put into operation that led us to consider reality in a certain way. Then, with time, those thoughts progressed, joined with other similar ones, and in the end became strong in our mind, in our consciousness, in a movement that then passed into our memory and there it remains in the form of messages that from time to time arise again, mixing with other similar ones.

Where messages are born

Many thoughts wander around, in our mind, because at a certain time we created them, they were joined with similar contents and these fragments were stored in the deepest part of our memory, which is like a deposit that has no end.

If we are careless, meaningless thoughts appear, contents that are not related, in an unconscious and mechanical movement that we do not control; these are the thoughts that frequently alter us.

They remain active, as long as we pay attention to them, and they are there, in our inner conversation, in our inner voice. Many of these thoughts are the cause of our distortion of reality. They are concentrated there, in that space of our consciousness that is always active and they change our vision of things, they propose us a model to follow, through that whisper, that constant rumor that is our inner voice, where the contents of our memory sprout persistently.

That is where the messages that we say to ourselves when we are alone are born. Many of these messages can be contradictory, they can vary from one moment to another, depending on the circumstances in which we are, and little by little they determine us, they mark the path to follow; they tell us how we have to name what we see, what we should feel at each moment.

All this is hidden there, in our inner voice, which is where the thoughts that we have in our mind at every moment are represented, while we dedicate ourselves to sustain them, to feed them in some way.

That is why they are sustained for long periods of time. The inner voice is like their refuge. Many of them do not have a concrete purpose or we do not understand them exactly, but they remain there, in the shadow.

To become aware of them

Only when we examine ourselves, we find enough clarity to realize all this, all these elements that manifest in our consciousness, in our inner voice. Some of which we are not able to decipher and which are executed without further ado, exerting an enormous influence on us, confusing us, influencing our understanding, our reasoning and judgments.

If we get a little distracted, we will allow ourselves to be manipulated, because we will end up acting according to the direction that they mark us.

If we are aware of all this, we will reach the source, the origin where everything is born; and once there, we can moderate this mechanism and reach clarity, which we will only obtain from tranquility, from calm.

If we are aware of this constant movement of our mind, in silence, we can realize how it works, the path that all those processes that we carry within us follow and that always try to find a way out, even if it is sometimes anguish or our own suffering.

13. Inner peace

If we move away from the noise of thoughts, we reach peace of mind. It is an inner peace that takes us to a clearer space, where we find the origin of all things, of what we are. Where there is neither suffering nor that constant murmur of your inner chatter that often takes over your reason.

When we feel liberated from it, nothing influences us anymore. We reach a serenity that protects us from confusion; we find an order within us that eliminates all suffering and at the same time makes us strong.

When inner peace penetrates you, that incessant voice in your head ends, it ceases to be maintained.

When your inner peace is intense, you do not let yourself be deceived by your mind, nor by all those thoughts that take possession of you falsifying the truth of things.

At that point there are no difficulties, no problems, everything is processed with a clarity that gives you an inner peace that you cannot guess until you experience it.

When you feel that you are at peace within you, there is an acceptance of the things that happen. You don't worry so much about the causes or the consequences of whatever is happening, you just accept it, trying not to let it influence you too much.

It is a way to govern yourself, to dominate all those internal conflicts and hostility inside you, product of the deception of the mind. Then, thanks to your inner voice, you establish another kind of communication with yourself that is more precise, more grounded, through a dialogue that is born of silence, of true knowledge, of what you are, that does not invent anything and that offers you the possibility of maintaining contact with something that exists beyond your own thoughts, that is on another level, in another deeper dimension, further away from the impressions of the mind.

PAUSE

We must observe from tranquility, establishing a pause, recovering that stillness necessary to regain control of ourselves. It is the only way to intervene on all that mental activity that many times disconcerts us without being able to establish an order within our internal world.

It is just a matter of stopping for a moment and seeing what thoughts occupy our consciousness at that moment. Immediately we will be able to make an evaluation of them, even if it is very quick and superficial.

It all depends on that, that we are aware, somehow, of that process that takes place within us and that often leads us to act by inertia, without thinking too much about what we do.

We can always count on the resource of conscious observation, which we can use if we can pause and direct our attention to all those elements that are causing us an oppression or anxiety at that moment.

For all this we only need to find that inner calm that we can only access through silence. We can create the conditions to reach it, to achieve that tranquility that separates us from any external influence and even from the mental noise that we constantly suffer.

Through practice we can achieve great progress in this sense. Once we acquire the habit, we will find it easier to enter our own inner world through stillness and silence.

In this way, we will access a new state of mind without thought: a space of our consciousness without objects, without images and without any other content that can divert our attention.

Putting the brakes on

We are not obliged to always have to think about something, it is possible to stop and make our mind go blank at certain times. In this way we will manage to open a space between each thought, in such a way that we will establish a certain distance between all that multitude of contents that constantly arise in our mind.

We will feel in those moments that we take control, somehow, of what we are thinking. When we stop all that stream of mental contents, we manage to have some time, even if it is brief, to order our internal discourse. If we manage to pause, we will have enough space to put aside those thoughts that do not benefit us, that we understand to be toxic for us.

If we have the habit of pausing daily, we will be able to somehow put a stop to this mechanism that tries to direct our own behaviors. We will learn to use the time we need to be aware that this is happening in our mind.

In this way we will be able to stop letting ourselves be carried away by the first thing that comes to our mind, by all those unconscious impulses that continuously overwhelm us and that many times end up dominating us without us being very conscious of it.

Select

In addition, we will have the opportunity to separate in some way everything that does not serve us, everything that we understand that can produce us some damage or an undesired consequence.

We will have the opportunity to choose the best possible response to all those difficulties that we face daily; since thanks to this pause that we can make, we will have the opportunity to select the best possible response, or at least the most coherent one: the one that is more related to what we really are.

Control

If I do not pause, the activity of my inner voice continues unchecked. If from serenity I do not limit its influence and manage to moderate it, it will not diminish, it will not be silenced; on the contrary, it will continue to sow discord through my own thoughts and will invite me to continue living in a false, dark reality, which is not the one that manifests itself on the outside.

We all need some time to pause, to somehow stop

this mental mechanism that leads us to behave in an unconscious way most of the time. It will always be beneficial for us to have a space where we can observe ourselves, to realize where we are heading.

If we find daily that space to see ourselves, to observe our own thoughts, we will have the opportunity to modify many aspects in our life that surely are not causing us any benefit. We will be more aware of all those negative and toxic thoughts that cause us harm without us realizing it.

In this way we will be able to establish a control over our own mind, because we will manage to take control of what happens there. It is just a matter of getting used to do a small daily meditation exercise, where we learn to be aware of everything that happens inside.

When I establish a pause I return to a state of calm, so that in those moments I feel that I am in control of what is happening.

So far it is the best formula I have found to achieve a certain mastery of myself. It consists of stopping, even for a few moments, to observe whatever is happening. At that moment you will understand if it is good for you or not. If it is not, you can intervene and change the direction of what you are thinking. You can divert your attention to another subject.

Conflicts disappear

Our inner voice will slowly disappear, because all those repetitive thoughts that constantly appear in our mind will fade away. A space will open up in which we will feel liberated in some way, because we will notice immediately that our conflicts, which are totally linked to our thoughts, will begin to disappear and cease to exert their influence.

Many thoughts run through our mind while they are creating an alteration that little by little is increasing, if we do not establish a pause so that this mechanism ends and other more positive thoughts are produced.

Therefore, if we are not conscious, we will let ourselves be directed by all these processes. If we do not evaluate what is happening, we will live in a constant suffering from which we will not be able to free ourselves so easily.

When we pause, we can observe all these impressions, all these traces of our consciousness, we become aware of those that can harm us. We can see how they evolve, how they wander through our mind, repeating themselves over and over again.

If we have the ability to escape from all this disturbance and return to stillness, we will observe that in that pause all the conflicts and all that suffering that is slowly disintegrating us, without us being very conscious of it, are eliminated.

This will have great benefits for our mental health. It will help us to resolve all those internal conflicts that we have been dragging for a long time.

You will realize

If you pause you will realize what you are thinking at that moment; you realize that your thoughts are like an endless train of images that do not stop circulating through your consciousness. Until you stop to observe what is going on inside you, you cannot stop it.

Usually we limit ourselves to follow them, to let ourselves be carried away by the stream of thoughts that arise there, constantly and repetitively. We can only reach a control, a mastery over this mechanism, if we establish a pause, if we stop to observe what is happening on that screen that is our consciousness.

Then we will realize that everything stops, that all those thoughts that cause us discomfort, suffering, stop having so much influence on us. It is as if, by observing, we feel relieved of the influence that our own mind has, through all those thoughts that arise from our memory.

If we stop, we can observe our inner voice, analyze its characteristics and the way it works. We can realize the power it has over us, that in most cases we remain unconscious and do not stop to observe what we are thinking, even if it leads us to disaster or has serious consequences in the future. If we achieve this, we somehow gain control of our own thoughts.

Finding oneself

Establishing a pause in due time, to be somewhat more aware of who we are, will allow us to find ourselves. This will help us to become aware of the reality in which we are living. He who comes to self-knowledge, succeeds in discovering the truth, the true reality in which he lives.

Then we will know if we are living in a fiction or if we are with our feet on the ground, in the authentic reality of life.

We can only know this if we are aware of everything that is going on in our head. It is possible if we have the ability to observe our own inner voice and to analyze its content, to see its origin and the consequences that can have all those elements that arise in our conscience that trap us completely and make us lead an unconscious life, far from the reality of life.

It will be a way to know ourselves much better and to find that reality that allows us to observe without judging, without putting previous labels.

CALM

When your calm becomes constant, you do not let yourself be carried away by everything that your thoughts suggest to you. There is something like an order within you that eliminates all restlessness, all affliction.

Through calmness we find equilibrium, through which all the mental activity to which we are accustomed is pacified.

In a state of calm you feel that you are not predetermined by anything, because there are hardly any judgments and reasonings; you only limit yourself to observe each element that arises, each content that is agitated by that vast space that is your consciousness, which sometimes distorts the truth of things, when you do not pay enough attention.

Therefore, it becomes necessary for us to look for that calmness to escape from fatality, from uncertainty, from that voice that subdues us and delimits us, introducing a certain way of thinking, conditioned by time.

If you have the privilege of finding your own inner calm, you will be able to contemplate what I am telling you; you will be able to understand how you function

inside; how that inner voice slows down and everything in your mind seems more organized. It is as if
you could go to the beginning, where it all begins, to
the origin, to the causes that have made you the person you are now.

A new order

We have to establish a new order through calmness.
We cannot subordinate ourselves to all those processes
that try to mark the path to follow in every moment.

We only have to observe all those expressions that
appear in our internal dialogue; in which there is little
clarity, because they are disordered or too negative.

If they are very insistent, we must move them away
by directing our point of attention to another place. It
will be the only way to recover our calm, which only
occurs when we do not let ourselves be impressed by
all those ideas that close the door on us, that rise up
and prevent us from being what we really are.

Within each of us is the will to establish a new order
in our inner world, to find, in this way, that peace that
can only be felt when we isolate ourselves from our
own thoughts, when we separate ourselves from all
that mental noise that often overwhelms us, inclining
us to do things we should not do.

In these cases we feel like a liberation. That inner
voice begins to suppress itself, while we let ourselves
be absorbed by silence. Then we reach stillness, thanks
to that pause that takes us away from confusion and
makes us aware of all that is moving inside; that we
control even our own impulses, which often rush us to
perform a lot of incoherent actions, which are not in

line with what we should really do.

It is the only way to diminish and shorten all that repetitive chatter that robs us of our calm, through an internal discourse that leads us to confusion and separates us from what we really are.

Thanks to stillness, everything becomes orderly, everything takes on a consonance. It is like going back to the beginning, where clarity becomes visible, because the consciousness is cleansed of all those contents that are lodged there, unconsciously, trying to put obstacles to your life.

Transcending the mind

If we are attentive to those thoughts, to that inner voice, we manage to stop all that mental activity; we manage to clean our consciousness a little bit of all those obstacles, of all those impediments that prevent us from reaching clarity and the true understanding of things.

We can only appreciate this from calm and tranquility, with a little willpower on our part, in a situation in which we observe ourselves. Then we will discover many secrets that are hidden within that inner world where everything originates.

We will be able, in some way, to stop all those attacks of our own unconscious impulses that often overflow us, making us grow a stream of thoughts that in the end end end up taking over us.

For this we must transcend our own mind: all those contents that are generated unconsciously. We can only achieve this if we manage to go beyond and free ourselves from all these conditioned thoughts that we have the habit of accepting without further ado, without being aware of the consequences that this entails.

Only in a situation of calm, of tranquility, we can make that leap to that other dimension, free of thoughts, where we find that peace necessary to give vent to what we really are, to discover the true beginning of all things, where everything begins.

As if everything stops

When this happens: when we flee from the din of the external world and look more inward, we find a certain harmony in our inner world, as if everything stops and there is nothing important, fundamental, to pay attention to.

In that inner calm that we achieve, we do not feel the obligation to focus on a particular thought, nor the need to be concerned about a particular problem. Everything becomes simpler, more uniform. Many of our habitual thoughts are interrupted, all those ideas that are constantly being integrated into our consciousness, trying to direct us, stop being elaborated.

We do not have to worry about trying to manage all those contents, to look for a meaning to each element that arises in our consciousness; it is as if everything returns to its right proportion.

Then our inner voice stops exclaiming, repeating all those repetitive thoughts stored in our memory and that in most cases we allow because we are not aware that this is happening.

Thanks to calmness you eliminate all the internal agitation that exists within you, you manage to postpone it for a while. It is as if everything stops and you pass to another state, as if you were located in another different place, where you have the faculty to observe yourself appreciating everything that happens in your consciousness, in such a way that you no longer feel predetermined by your own thoughts, by the urgency of your mind to always look for a concept, an image or an idea to capture your attention. It is as if you were moving away from all that vertiginous mental activity that subdues you and tries to dominate you from beginning to end.

From tranquility I feel that I can stop all this mechanism, all this machinery that reproduces in me the same confusion, the same anguish.

We see in a more precise way

If we move away a little and separate ourselves from the contamination of our own thoughts, we can experience a calmness that little by little brings order to the chaos that often reigns in our inner world.

When we reach it, we see everything in a more precise way and many things stop hurting us, since we become more aware of the information that circulates in those moments in our mind. It is as if we come out of the darkness of the shadows and reach a reality that makes us see the truth in all its dimension.

It is important that we return to that calm that makes us see things in a different way, with greater objectivity. Our judgments and our way of interpreting reality will be much more rational and closer to the truth. We will not let ourselves be carried away by all those unconscious impulses that cloud our reason.

You move away from all influences

From the calm, when I find myself away from all external influences, I feel that an inner peace blooms in me that takes me away from all the commotion that exists outside and the noise that my own mind causes through all those contents that arise constantly and repetitively in my consciousness.

If we move away a little from all those external influences that we have to endure daily, we will see that within us a calmness will spread that will eliminate our worries, somehow extinguishing our daily problems.

All this happens when we move away from the external noise, from all those stimuli that we find outside and that many times disorient us, because they capture our attention while they are being reproduced.

When we do not let ourselves be exalted by all that is outside, in our immediate environment, the intensity of all those stimuli begins to diminish; it becomes weaker as time goes by.

At that moment we begin to observe ourselves, since from that tranquility we begin to consider that other world that exists inside; to which we rarely pay attention, since we are more aware of the external reality that occurs outside and that somehow determines our habits and our behaviors.

When you reach stillness, you move away from all influence, from all that mental noise that accumulates inside you and that ends up driving you.

In stillness, your inner dialogue is not subject to the first thing that comes to your mind, nor is it influenced by the past, nor is it affected by what may happen in the future. There is no permanent discussion within you, of contradictory ideas trying to place themselves in your consciousness.

We feel a liberation

When all that mental activity compresses and squeezes us, we must diminish its vivacity and find the inner peace that protects us from all that torrent of impulses and mental stimuli.

Thanks to this inner peace, we feel a liberation, because somehow we abandon the thoughts that always try to absorb us, calling our attention. All begins to occupy the calm and silence, and from there we can contemplate that there is a fascinating world where there is no confusion, but the pause and tranquility.

In it a calmness spreads that makes us aware of everything that arises in our mind. Entering this state is like an awakening, where we can discover ourselves, beyond the clutter of the mind.

It is important that we get used to experience this feeling of inner calm, since thanks to it we can separate ourselves from all those obstacles that create conflicts within ourselves.

In a way, our mood at any given moment depends on putting an end to that voice, on freeing ourselves from that internal dialogue that sometimes isolates us from reality.

Achieving serenity

We only have to reach serenity, with patience, in this way we will put an end to the restlessness that we may experience internally. Thanks to it we protect ourselves, we reach the control of everything that develops in our mind in every moment.

On the other hand, if we let ourselves be carried away by the agitation, this will be prolonged in time and will be mixed with other ailments, in such a way that we will feel a confusion that little by little will precipitate us to the emptiness.

If we seek and achieve serenity, we will reach sanity, which will cure our suffering and all that avalanche of conflicts that continually overflow us.

From serenity we can detach ourselves from the darkness of the mind, which on many occasions torments us with images that incite us to abandon the reality that surrounds us and to create an alternative world, in which in the end we end up submerging ourselves, due to the movement of the mind and the agitation that exists there.

It becomes necessary to seek serenity; it is the most convenient thing to do when we experience some confusion. When we achieve it, we return to that inner calm where our inner world is illuminated and all those mental manifestations cease to appear.

Only from serenity can we orient all these processes that we can only appreciate thanks to the conscious observation of that inner voice, which is nothing more than the reflection of all those mental representations that are created in our consciousness, many times in an imprecise, indefinite and confusing way.

Once we recover serenity, we can discover many things that are hidden, but that do not come to light because of the increase of other kinds of thoughts to which we give relevance.

Serenity is only sustained in that calm that is created within, when the torments of our own mind disappear;

when we go beyond our own thoughts and go deeper than what is merely observable, and we separate ourselves somehow from all that mental activity in which we are continuously secluded and go to another level, from where we can examine everything with much greater clarity, because we have the calm and enough time to observe how our reasoning is based, how our judgments are created, which in reality are the origin of all those strange confusions that emanate from our mind that are rapidly accelerated throughout our consciousness.

In serenity everything seems more in accordance, more sensible, I do not feel determined by anything. From tranquility you see things in a different way. The inner workings are different, one seems to be more optimistic, more self-aware.

One's own reasoning seems less confused; this helps to reach true understanding, which quickly dissolves the disorder and all those complications of life that often affect us to such an extent that we allow ourselves to be dominated by them, allowing them to be prolonged in time.

To look from the emptiness

Stop judging everything you see, everything you think. Stop sowing confused interpretations of everything you observe. Just limit yourself to look from the void, from that space far away from the mind where there are no events or issues of the past, because there is only an interval of silence that extends to the depths of yourself and leads you to the understanding of all things, of what you are, away from all those imaginary thoughts that your own mind proposes at every step. All this can only happen in calm, in tranquility, without anything that can harm you, harm you.

When you observe everything from that space, you find an inner peace that makes you feel free, far from the constant struggle that exists in your own mind, where you only find obstacles that lead you to confusion on many occasions.

If you observe all this carefully, you will be able to discover all those signals that come from deep inside yourself and that lead you to what you really are.

14. Silence

Within us lies a hidden secret. It can only be accessed through silence. All you have to do is stop - there is no set duration for this - and observe everything that shows up in your mind: all the elements that flood it.

If you find yourself in a situation of silence, you will realize that all that confusion begins to shift, to move to another place. Then the thoughts stop associating, become less powerful and disappear.

A change originates within you, because your consciousness begins to experience an emptiness, so that your judgments disappear and it is as if everything begins to purify. Your daze, to which you are accustomed, begins to disappear and your inner voice stops murmuring through all those thoughts that are repeated unconsciously; and a clarity begins to be exhibited in your consciousness that is increasing, as calmness reigns within you.

It is enough for us not to abandon that silence that inclines us to establish a communication with ourselves, to create a secret dialogue with what we really are.

OVERCOMING OBSTACLES

Thanks to silence, I have learned to overcome obstacles, to be above difficulties. I have felt light, liberated from the daze. I have managed to understand the inexplicable; to be aware of myself, of what I really am. It seems as if all uncertainties disappear in that state. The benefits I have gained from silence are indisputable.

Whenever I feel that something is contaminating me inside, I turn to it. It helps me to dig deeper inside myself, to discover the cause of what I am experiencing at any given moment. In this way I can see clearly, in a serene way, what I am thinking.

When we manage to create an atmosphere of silence, the conflicts that usually surround you disappear. They cease to spread, because thanks to stillness you establish a rupture with everything that subdues you, that alters you, that tries to transform you into what you are not. In that instant you accept reality as it is, without putting any kind of resistance, reaching mental balance.

Through silence you can fix a little bit all that disorder that happens in your mind, because you isolate yourself from the mental noise and it weakens and somehow you separate yourself from that disorganized and automatic mechanism that constantly slides through your mind a series of elements that are composing your way of seeing the world, your way of understanding reality. Silence is a good tool to achieve this.

You find a rest that makes you postpone all those worries you feel in your daily life, because all the conflicts begin to diminish, they cease to have meaning for you, because you do not feel the need to focus on them.

At that moment adversities disappear, conflicts stop passing through our mind, while we manage to conquer the mastery of ourselves through that stillness that leads us on a path where there is only peace and a freedom that makes us independent, far from the darkness of the mind, from uncertainties and suffering.

When this happens all difficulties disappear. It is as if all problems are suspended in time and your mind comes out of the darkness and reaches understanding; but first you need to make this journey: you have to remain in silence, which will make everything stop, even that inner speech that you repeat to yourself constantly and that ends up guiding you without you hardly being aware of it.

WE CAN OBSERVE

One of the ways to appease our inner voice is through silence. In this way we can clearly appreciate everything that is manifesting inside. We can inspect it in more detail and establish a distance with any element that tries to envelop us.

Thanks to silence we can clearly observe everything that happens, we can discover how the mechanism that envelops us works, that makes us uneasy through a succession of images that run through our mind influencing our mood, trying to dominate us, contaminating our consciousness and establishing a permanent discomfort.

Thanks to silence I have learned to dwell in more detail on all those manifestations that arise in my own mind, which often belong more to the world of my own imagination than to reality.

If you abandon yourself to it, you can clearly see everything that is projected in your consciousness, all that exposition of elements, that internal discourse that is stretched by your mind trying to subdue you.

Thanks to silence you find many advantages, because it gives you the faculty to be a little absent from ordinary life and to observe things from another point of view, as if from a more distanced point of view. In this way you move away from confusion, because everything seems to stop in this state.

In those moments you will begin to create another way of seeing the world much more natural, without falsehoods or deceptions, without feeling dominated by any influence. Thanks to silence you will obtain all these benefits, you will examine everything with different eyes, with a much more radiant look.

When you abandon yourself in silence, away from all preoccupation, the activity of your mind diminishes, it softens, so to speak. Your intellect becomes more rational, because you place yourself at a higher level of consciousness, from which you can observe with tranquility all that can stun you, all those thoughts that often lead you to deception, when they suddenly arise in your consciousness and take hold of your understanding and become constant.

A MEANS OF TRANSFORMATION

The wisdom of time has helped me to understand the hidden messages behind silence. It inspires me, helps me to find transformation when I need it, producing changes in me that are impossible to experience in any other way.

It is a good tool to reestablish the lost order within you, to rebuild yourself inside and repair all those areas damaged by your own suffering.

Thanks to it you will connect with yourself, through that bond that can only be established within that space away from the noise of the mind.

When I step back a little and take a break, through silence, I limit myself to observe all those ideas that circulate restlessly through my own interior. In those moments it is as if everything is postponed, I do not let myself be carried away by my impulses.

My inner voice softens and a great space of inner calm is created in me that helps me to transform myself into what I really am, which is something that is beyond the mind. It is something that has to do with my true nature, which is always calm and does not allow itself to be overwhelmed by noise: by that disorder that many times there is within me, that confuses me, that little by little weakens me, when I do not understand it and do not find clarity.

Therefore, we could say that silence is healing, because it gradually heals our emotional wounds, the negative memories of the past and all those negative beliefs about the world and about ourselves.

As there are no thoughts, nothing can influence you negatively, nothing can affect you. You will feel distanced from any toxic element that may be inside you, in your memory, in your unconscious.

You will only feel that you are there, with yourself, limiting yourself to observe the silence and all that immense space that is your consciousness without objects, without thoughts, without anything that can harm you.

YOU FIND INNER PEACE

I have found enough patience to penetrate into my inner world and let myself be transported by that inner peace that can only be experienced in temperance, when one totally escapes from the external noise and also from the din of one's own thoughts.

One must abandon oneself in silence to seek the necessary tranquility. Only at that moment can you contemplate the emptiness within you, where thoughts stop racing and you manage to establish a cohesion with yourself.

If you know how to appreciate silence, you will find inner peace, which eliminates suffering, which cancels all those negative thoughts that irritate you.

THE ENTRANCE TO ANOTHER DIMENSION

Many thoughts stop coming together, slowly begin to fade away and many mental representations stop influencing you, while you remain present, focused on everything that moves within you, attending to each manifestation and trying to go beyond, towards that other hidden dimension where there is no alteration and you experience an inner peace that takes you away from the noise of the mind and makes you be present, under the amazement of all that formless space where everything begins, where the beginning of what we are and the basis of what we will become in the future is found.

Thanks to silence you move away from the dominion of your own mind, so that you settle in another space, in another dimension where you stop acting, where nothing leads you anymore.

In those moments you stop being determined by your own mind, you stop being subjected to your own thoughts.

You have the opportunity to enter another dimension, as if you were passing to another level where all those constant thoughts stop reproducing themselves.

An encounter with your spiritual part is established, where you find the balance that you do not get anywhere else. Many of your ideas, judgments and reasonings stop being associated all at once, stop dominating you, stop conquering your mental space that invade you daily, that numb you and make you unconscious, turning you into a machine that tries to execute a series of behaviors in a mechanical way, related to all those mental representations that are incorporated in a repetitive way to your consciousness.

Silence is beneficial for you, because in it you find a calmness that leads you to balance, to moderation. It is the entrance to your spiritual part, where you find clarity and understanding of all that you do not usually understand.

15. Balance

If you manage to orient your thoughts properly, you will never move away from reality, you will not have the need to create new representations through the use of your own imagination. You will observe everything as it is, nothing will separate you from the truth.

When you look closely at the whole world that dwells within you, you will discover an extraordinary potential that will rebuild everything that is damaged within you. Nothing will bring you down, nothing will upset you, because you will be able to clearly distinguish which thoughts are the most appropriate for you.

It is the only way to reestablish balance in our own mind; the only way to make our judgments more sensible; to establish order in all that internal structure that we are building little by little, often unconsciously; It is the only way to get away from confusion, from mental darkness, from everything that inclines us not to be ourselves, from everything that robs us of calm and does not allow us to develop our best qualities, which only emerge in those moments when we connect with what we really are, when we observe reality as it is, away from mental noise and those toxic thoughts that try to join all those messages that we tell ourselves when we use our internal dialogue to talk to ourselves.

Sometimes we sink into the abyss in an incomprehensible way. We let ourselves be guided by our powerful mind, by all that movement, that activity where some thoughts are associated with others in such a way that they gradually increase.

If we have the ability to appropriate this mechanism, we will establish equilibrium. All those thoughts will diminish our difficulties, which will be resolved little by little.

It is not easy to reach equilibrium. It comes when you reach mental clarity, when you do not allow yourself to be overwhelmed or enveloped by mental conflicts.

Balance begins when calm is established within you and you begin to master yourself. Then you discover that there is a power within you that makes you reach understanding, as soon as you meditate for a few moments and focus on what only brings you well-being.

At that moment is when the balance is manifested. It is when you move away from confusion and come to true knowledge: to a hidden wisdom that begins to accompany you and is like a coat, because thanks to it you come to understand the reality as it is: that which is far from all appearances, which does not deceive you and that is in the depths of yourself.

If we do not let ourselves be carried away by our inner voice, we will find balance, which will only come about if we put aside all those deceptive and annoying components that often prevent us from seeing reality as it is.

ESTABLISH A DISTANCE

Sometimes we talk to ourselves. We have an internal talk about life or any other circumstance we are living in those moments.

We begin to collect thoughts that are lying around in the deepest recesses of our memory. We put them together and create mental representations that stay with us for long periods of time.

Once we constitute a series of ideas about life and the world, they begin to repeat themselves continuously in our head. We relate them to each other, when they are similar, and in this way we create a vision of things that in the end determines us. What we think is what ends up guiding us without us realizing it.

It is advisable, from time to time, to establish a certain distance from our own thoughts. We can change our view of things in this way.

It is a way to restore balance to our inner world, which we sometimes lose because we feel induced by beliefs that we have created for ourselves and that end up remaining within us for long periods of time.

BENEFITS

Trying to maintain mental balance is always beneficial, because it provides you with a calm space where you can examine your own mental activity, so that you can observe what kind of contents feed your thoughts and all those related emotions that are leaving an impression inside you.

It helps you to abandon that feeling of frustration that sometimes sets in when we prove that what we have thought does not conform to reality. When you put everything in its place in your mind, you will always go in the right direction, there will be no division in you or lack of coherence. You will find clarity, so that everything you think will be right, will have a reason to be and will keep you away from confusion, from all those irrational ideas that often lead to that feeling of frustration that makes us feel lost, because it penetrates into the deepest part of ourselves.

When you achieve balance, you are insensitive to the deception of your own thoughts, because you just observe, with nothing to drive you to action, with nothing to encourage you or spread inside you trying to divert your attention.

Maintaining balance helps you to be closer to the truth, to not adulterate the reality of what you see, since you observe everything from tranquility, from a stillness that leads you to pay attention to what really matters, only to those aspects that are in line with who you are, with what you really want to do.

To live in balance is to be coherent with oneself; it is not to let oneself be carried away by the current, by all that whirlwind of external influences that often force us to change direction, to interrupt our course, letting ourselves be carried away by the force of external stimuli, to which we are often subjected without realizing it.

Mental balance gives us depth, helps us to be more in touch with what we really are.

It encourages us to establish a communication with that more hidden part that is further away from thought, from the noise of the mind. So one becomes more authentic, thanks to that distance that is created with the automatic mind, with all those processes that subject us, that limit us without often there is a moderation on our part.

16. Clarity

When this inner voice disappears, there is a pause where everything is ordered and there is no confusion. Then clarity appears. We come out of the darkness of the mind, as if we find the illumination that extends throughout our consciousness.

If we move away from that inner voice we will put a little more clarity in our mind and move away from all those irrational thoughts that are activated in our consciousness and try to evolve on their own.

I can see with clarity everything that is reproduced in my mind, even all those impulses that in many occasions lead me to behave in a certain way.

Then I feel I have the ability to flee from fatality, as if everything that causes me bitterness or sadness disappears. In those moments a clarity spreads within me that erases all those impressions of the past, that in many occasions are established in my conscience, sowing an impetuous restlessness.

It is important that we learn to renew ourselves from within, putting aside all those elements and replacing them with other more positive ones. It is a matter of always having clarity shining in our mind, a positive way of seeing the world.

For this it is necessary to renew some thoughts that

try to create disturbances in our own mind, in our own reason, in our way of seeing the world.

THANKS TO CONSCIOUSNESS

When I remain motionless, without establishing a link with the outside that can distract me, clarity arises in my mind, which brings great benefits to me.

In that state I feel that I abandon all outside influences. Then serenity absorbs me and I stop and I am aware in those moments of the situation I am in, of what I need to improve, of how all things are initiated. I can see the evolution in my own life, why it has gone in one direction and not another.

Thanks to mindfulness a clarity is created in our mind that makes us contemplate information in a more detailed way. It is as if in our intelligence there is a harmony that allows us to easily find the explanations we need to understand what we are seeing before us, to discover what is happening within ourselves.

We will reach the very basis of our own reasoning and we will discover which are erroneous and which are closer to the truth, to the objectivity of things. We will reach, in this way, clarity in our ideas, so we will know how to respond perfectly to each and every one of the difficulties of life and we will opt for the best decisions, at every moment; without being influenced by the deception of our own mind, by all those negative thoughts that try to keep us away from the truth, from the reality of things, from the world in which we live.

If we know how to appreciate this, we will come to know precisely what it is that harms us, what it is that triggers our suffering or what inclines us to separate ourselves from what we really are.

BENEFITS

Clarity allows you to analyze the secrets that are kept inside you, thus discovering the entrance door to that place where you really are.

With clarity, problems disappear, since your reason becomes stable and is only limited to see reality as it is, without deviating from what you really are.

Clarity does not need to seek any thought to establish its dominance. It does not lead you to conjectures or suspicions, it is freed from the bonds of the mind; it does not enter into that game.

It does not need to go to the memories of the past to distinguish itself. In it only the truth is preserved, and an order that takes control of your consciousness and strengthens your own understanding.

We reach a state of no suffering, of no affliction, because we do not experience the dominion of thoughts, the deception of our own mind, through that incessant murmuring, that inner chatter that slowly beats us.

In those moments, your thoughts do not take a concrete direction; you feel that clarity takes hold of you, which makes you feel a relief that leads you to experience an inner calm that takes you away from the usual convulsion that you experience in your mind, in a habitual way.

UNDERSTANDING

We have to understand reality, what is really happening, in order to know how to orient ourselves. The amount of information that reaches us is immense, so we must examine it well to keep what is really useful to us.

Each situation leaves us with a new teaching, a new learning. Our intellect captures it and stores it for when we need it, introducing that information in our memory.

All this stored material will help us to understand later what we do not understand. We will be able to associate knowledge through reflection, and in this way we will reach the understanding of the facts that happen to us or those that we observe around us.

In this way our reason is founded, which is concerned with seeking evidence to find an explanation for those things that remain beyond our own understanding.

In this way we are able to solve all those difficulties that come our way. We will always find a reasoning that will illuminate the way. We only have to try to observe a little, and our intelligence will find clarity, if there is darkness in us.

Thanks to our own reasoning, we can guess what may happen. We will have no difficulty in foreseeing the future, if we know how to discover the causes behind everything that happens.

We only need to show a certain interest in seeing how our reason works, how it tries to associate thoughts through our own reflections.

If we explore a little inside ourselves, we will be able

to discover it. We will see how we create our own ideas, how we give continuity to a certain way of thinking, without being very conscious of the consequences it may have.

When we become aware in every situation of what is happening, we come to understand it, we reach an understanding that makes us draw the right conclusions; even if we see many difficulties.

If we reach the comprehension of everything that happens to us, we will move away from confusion and we will find clarity. We will stop sowing doubt and a space will open up in our consciousness where we will always find the truth.

If we come to understand why things happen - the reasons why a series of events occur - we will discover the causes that have led us to the situation we are in. The circumstances in which we live are nothing more than the consequences of all our previous actions.

Going a little further

To understand reality it is necessary that we penetrate a little further, that we look for the true meaning of things and not get carried away by the stream of thoughts that arise immediately and that have to do more with what appearances are and not with what is hidden behind, with what each object and each thing that we observe really is.

Paying attention to our inner voice has these benefits: to observe and come to an understanding of everything that manifests in our consciousness.

If you ask yourself questions about the things that happen, trying to find an explanation to all those manifestations that occur outside, you can understand the events, situations and all that confusion that often hovers around us and remains for a long time there, waiting for us to find a solution.

If we observe ourselves, we can clarify many doubts about how we are. We can reach understanding and discover a great number of qualities that are hidden from our inner perception that we cannot notice because our attention is only focused on what our mind is proposing at any given moment.

17. Control

When we gain control of ourselves, everything changes in our inner world. We come to feel a greater security, a greater confidence in everything we do, since in this way we can achieve a coherence between what we think and what we really are.

The starting point is that content that arises in our mind and that manages to catch us and direct and change the direction of our actions and behaviors. It has so much power over us that it has the capacity to make us change direction, to make us stop doing a certain act and immediately start doing another action.

That is why it is important to at least try to exercise some control over our own thoughts, because they form the basis of what we end up doing at every moment of our lives.

CONSTANT ACTIVITY

There is constant activity within us. We cannot reduce it so easily, since it is composed of a series of impetuous stimuli that do not have any type of regulation on our part and they are deciding the contents that have to arise in our mind.

This one is arranging them without any type of order, as they are presented. Little by little, these elements are accommodated in our consciousness and increase as they are repeated, until they manage to appropriate our attention. They somehow manage to awaken our interest, although many of these contents are not faithful to the truth -they may contain misleading impressions about reality-, since many of these elements are nothing more than the product of our own imagination.

They slowly take hold of us, through all those representations that flourish in our mind. Some of them can be unpleasant, because they contain negative images from the past; they make us lose our peace of mind, because in some way they revive the memory of previous bad experiences, lengthening the load of negativity of past experiences that were not pleasant.

This kind of content remains in time, even if it is very distant. It is what feeds all those toxic thoughts that confuse us and make us lose our way, in many occasions.

IMPULSIVE MECHANISM

When thoughts are triggered, the balance in the deepest part of oneself is broken. Everything happens very fast, without us noticing it. Many contents are executed in an impetuous way and once they start, it is difficult to stop them. Then they accumulate, associating with each other, and they gain strength at the same time that they take away our peace of mind.

All this movement that agitates us internally rushes upon us without us realizing it, because we remain ignorant, most of the time, of these processes that are accelerated in our mind and that in the end generate confusion.

It is an impulsive mechanism that tries to look for alternatives among all those contents that we have stored in our memory. Little by little some are turned on and others are turned off, but it gives the impression that it is an activity that never ends, it seems that it is always in an active state that never decreases.

WE MUST ANTICIPATE

In order to have a clear vision of what is happening in our mind, we have to try to diminish all these elements that rise from our memory and try to amplify themselves in our consciousness, repeating themselves over and over again.

We cannot allow them to spread, if these kinds of contents are not healthy, if they lead us to anguish, sadness or any other kind of agitation. We cannot allow them to confuse us.

We must anticipate this process of constant representations, sometimes the fruit of our own imagination, so as not to allow all these manifestations that lead us to anguish to emerge.

If we do not pay attention to this, we will allow them to accumulate in such a way that it is more difficult to get rid of them.

If we manage to moderate this mechanism, we will be able to appease all that fire that burns inside us in the form of repetitive thoughts that rob us of our calm.

We have to learn to keep our distance so as not to fall into the deception of our own mind. For this it is necessary to know this mechanism that separates us from what we really are, from our true essence.

OBSERVING

Our inner world is an unknown world. Only those who observe themselves, who look at themselves and free themselves in some way from all those external influences that often confuse us, have the privilege of knowing it.

He who observes himself, realizes what agitates him within; therefore it is difficult for him to let himself sink, to let himself be deceived by his own mind, for he has the opportunity to see perfectly what afflicts him at every moment.

He who is aware of all this, perceives how his inner voice reproduces itself, and in the end finds the way to silence it through silence.

Everything that spreads within can dominate us, if we do not exercise adequate control and manage to establish an order in all that creates division.

There are certain thoughts that can destroy us, if they are repeated too often in our mind and are toxic, if they are connected with others that are also toxic.

In these cases we must try to suppress them as quickly as possible; clean our mind of everything that is consuming us.

The best way is to observe them, being aware of the influence they exert. In order for them to finally change direction, we have to stop identifying with them, not getting too involved with what we are seeing in our consciousness in such a repetitive way. If we decide to carry out some activity so that our attention changes direction, we will see that all those thoughts will slowly disappear, separating from each other, as if they were leaving us in those moments.

The mind is a mechanism that forces us to act automatically, but we have the possibility to reject this option and take control. In those moments we have the mastery, so to speak, we do not allow ourselves to be enveloped by the deception of our own mind.

Only if we become aware of these kinds of processes can we slow them down, numb them. So depending on the level of observation that we have, many of these automatic thoughts begin to move to another place and little by little they are suppressed.

In this way we can take control, if we get used to examine what we are thinking at a given moment, which appears in our inner voice and that we can moderate in some way, if we put a little will on our part.

If we learn to exercise control over our own mind, controlling what we observe in our consciousness, we can somehow direct our own thoughts, organize our ideas, review many of our beliefs, many of which may not be accurate, may be wrong, since they are based on mere subjective interpretations that we once made about a series of facts that we had the opportunity to experience.

Observing the inner voice

We have to observe our inner voice, because it summarizes everything we think at any given moment.

We will become aware of the elements that are most repeated and that most influence us in our way of seeing reality, in our way of interpreting the world.

All this appears in our internal dialogue, in that conversation that we usually have with ourselves when no one is around us. It is there where we can notice that which tries to stun us, that which tries to disorient us and which produces an internal disorder.

Once we come to the knowledge of all this, we can exercise a certain mastery. Then we will find calm and sobriety. If we attend to all this we can exercise control over these processes, and therefore they will cease to affect us if we succeed.

We will manage, in this way, to direct our attention towards other kinds of thoughts that are more positive and more coherent with what we want to be and what we want to do.

It is simply a matter of doing an exercise of conscious observation, being attentive to that voice that repeats itself in our head in the form of thoughts. We will control, in some way, that internal dialogue that we have. It is a way of gaining control of our internal world. If we manage to direct that personal communication that exists inside, we will establish, in some way, a control over our own thoughts, over our way of thinking in certain situations.

All this we can achieve if we reach that internal control; and this can only be done based on the knowledge we acquire of these internal mechanisms that make us function in a certain way and that many times take us away from what we really are.

We can only acquire it through the observation of our own internal processes and our inner voice, which collects all those thoughts that are constantly circulating in our mind and shows it to us, in such a way that it gets us to put our focus of attention there, so that in the end it ends up determining us, influencing our way of doing things, in our vision of reality and in the relationships that we get to maintain with others.

BEING AWARE

If we are aware of this inner voice that we all have, we can delimit it; prevent it from dominating us, thus establishing an order that can lead us to decide what we want to think in each situation.

If we are conscious, we will not be governed by our own mind, we will not give continuity to its dominion, nor to that internal discourse that repeats itself so many times and that in many occasions takes us away from our own reality.

We will concentrate only on what is truly important; and we will feel liberated from the dominion of the mind, thus achieving an internal balance that will help us to reach the truth.

To achieve this, we only need to be aware of this mechanism, which is already implanted and is maintained by our own nature.

Although this is so, we can intervene and modify some aspects that have to do with this process. We will achieve great results if we try.

We will become aware of what drives us to act in a certain direction, of what captures our attention and changes the direction of our actions. Once we achieve this, we will feel liberated from this mechanism that somehow dominates us inside without us knowing it.

We can carry out a certain control, a dominion that establishes an order and a separation of those contents that can be harmful. The only way to achieve this is to be aware of it, that this exists and of the consequences of not being aware of these elements.

In this way we will manage to dominate, in some way, our mind and all those contents that appear in it; and also all those impulses that in many occasions arise suddenly and that trap us in such a way that we allow ourselves to be led by them.

REFLECTING

When I reflect, in a sensible way, on everything that limits me, on all those plots that I have in my head that in many occasions disturb me, I feel that I reach the domain of everything that extends in my mind and confuses me.

Just by looking at what I am thinking, making a small interval, I can clearly observe what it is that drags me to confusion, to anguish. I manage to realize that my mental activity is moving, trying to make some changes in me, disturbing my tranquility, leading me to distress.

I can clearly perceive how certain thoughts -which are nothing more than small fragments of the past-, are being placed in my consciousness, occupying a main position, sowing contrariness, contaminating everything that is there, everything that is around.

Then I am aware that, if I do nothing to avoid it, they can remain there for a long period of time. So I feel the need to purify that space, to consider other alternatives, to change reality, to focus on other more credible and cleaner thoughts. When I achieve this, I experience again the calm, the power of stillness that, once it remains fixed and lasts in time, helps me to get out of the chaos, to suppress everything that tries to obscure my vision of reality.

I cannot separate myself from what I think, but my experience has led me to the conclusion that I can re-direct many ideas that circulate in my mind, making them change their meaning, so that they do not enlarge those negative contents that often rush impulsively try-ing to park themselves in my consciousness.

When I achieve this, I feel that I have the control of myself; I appreciate that I have the capacity to be above everything that may disturb me at any given moment.

SETTING A DIRECTION

It is easy to get distracted by things that lead us no-where. If we can focus on what really matters, we will come to understand why things happen to us; to know the causes behind who we are.

When we achieve this, we can say that we are our-selves, because at that moment we are the ones who direct, in some way, our thoughts, our mind; and, therefore, we are the ones who mark at that moment the direction to follow. We do not let ourselves be car-ried away by that stream of ideas that circulate through our mind in a repetitive and mechanical way.

Once we take control, we have to know where to go, set a certain direction that is in relation and in ac-cordance with what we really are, with what we intend to be, with our true purpose, with what we understand that we must do to feel that we are ourselves and, therefore, to act with coherence; so that there is no distance between what we think and what we end up doing; so that everything goes in line.

If we let ourselves be carried away by the repetitive thoughts that our mind constantly proposes to us, our actions do not have a concrete purpose. We simply do things by inertia, without thinking too much; we execute them as if we were a robot, in a mechanical way, without even reflecting on the consequences they may have.

It is only a matter of gaining mental mastery, control of our own thoughts. If we manage to stop them from directing us, they will not lead us where they want us to go, nor will we end up doing the actions they determine.

If we take control of our own mind, everything we think and the actions that derive from those thoughts, will be produced in a conscious way -we will know exactly their purpose and the consequences they may have-; because at all times we will be in control, we will perceive where we are going and the purpose of everything we do.

In those moments everything changes: our behaviors begin to be different, so that everything we do from that moment on has a goal, a determined end.

LET IT GO

We must be careful with all that is expanded in our mind, sometimes it may not be beneficial. It depends on the kind of content in question. If they are toxic elements, it is clear that we have to put them aside in some way.

Any thought, no matter how insignificant it may seem, has its influence, both positively and negatively. There are thoughts that can create mental obstacles that prevent us from making decisions, from carrying out the appropriate actions to solve some difficulties that arise in our daily life.

Other kinds of thoughts can rob us of our happiness, our emotional well-being, if they are related to negative aspects of our past, to painful memories or to circumstances that we did not resolve properly at the time.

All this can rush over us without us realizing it, in a way that can darken our mind and make us lose clarity, which is what allows us to know what is most appropriate in each situation, in each circumstance.

The only way to deal with them is to be aware of them and not give them too much importance. The best thing to do is to let them pass, so that they do not spread in our mind and do not join with other similar ones. In this way they will begin to diminish and stop influencing us.

If we look at our own thoughts, we will discover which are the contents that we must stop, set aside. The only way to isolate them is to be attentive to everything that arises in our consciousness, that is deposited there, and that then appears in that inner voice that we all have through which all those contents that are fixed in our mind are repeated over and over again.

If we manage not to make them habitual, they will not absorb us, nor will they surprise us. They will not create confusion nor will they force us to carry out a certain action, since we will not be giving them the importance they demand. In this way they will stop accumulating one after another, so that they will keep us away from suffering and from all that anguish that many times we suffer and that does not disappear so easily, because once it takes root it remains for long periods of time, progressing slowly until it causes us an internal disorder that makes us live in confusion.

FREEDOM

Authentic freedom begins when we are the ones who decide what to think about; when we do not let ourselves be carried away by our own mind, which is usually the one that proposes the contents to which we must pay attention.

We are free when we have the opportunity to decide on which thoughts to focus our gaze; and within those, which are the important ones. When we have the opportunity to choose the type of action we consider most appropriate at any given moment.

We are really free when we reach the control and mastery of ourselves; when we do not allow our own unconscious mechanisms to have the command of our internal world.

18. Change

If we know how to find an explanation for our own behaviors, we can establish the changes we need at any given moment. In this way our actions will have an order, they will be more coherent with what we really want to do deep inside ourselves. They will not be as involuntary as usual.

To do all this with ease, it is necessary that we pay attention to what happens first in our consciousness. We should not limit ourselves to listening to that inner voice that repeats itself over and over again, because that is where all those thoughts are found that in the end end end up dominating us and creating a mental programming that in the end becomes habits that are difficult to eliminate.

Many of the difficulties are found inside, in that mental space where our ideas are produced, where our decisions really begin, when we face each of the circumstances that we have to live. If we gain control of that area, we can somehow control everything that manifests itself there. We can clearly observe the activity that happens there, so that we will be in a very good position to make the appropriate changes, so that in the end our mind does not have so much influence over us.

It is a matter of changing direction when necessary. The best way is to suspend that mental mechanism, many times unconscious, that often invites us to go in a certain direction, which sometimes we are not the ones who choose it.

ANALYZE THE REASONS

If we know how to situate ourselves at the beginning, where our actions begin, we will observe that an action is nothing more than the maturation of a series of thoughts that have been constantly repeated in our mind. These thoughts have acquired such a dimension that in the end they have become a specific behavior that we carry out. If we repeat this behavior over time, it will lead to the creation of a habit. If that habit is harmful, if it is not healthy for us, it will eventually create problems for us.

If certain habits begin to create difficulties for us and we come to the conclusion that we have made a mistake, promoting those certain behaviors, we will be able to find some kind of solution and we will try to get rid of those behaviors, which we execute repeatedly and which are not beneficial.

This can only happen if we observe ourselves, if we reflect a little and deliberately examine the situation we are in at that moment. In this way we will be able to analyze the reasons that have led us to the situation in which we find ourselves in each circumstance. If it is not good, we will try to come up with some kind of solution.

FEELING THE NEED

It can also happen that we get used to certain routines, so we do not feel the need to have to change, so we can stay for long periods of time with the same habits, simply because we have become accustomed to them and we are not aware at that time of the negative consequences they may have for us later.

When we experience a situation in which we begin to encounter many inconveniences and numerous difficulties, then we do not postpone any longer the decision to make some changes. Then we try to moderate what has gotten out of hand.

We consider, in such a situation, that we cannot continue like this and that we have to change, in some way, our lifestyle or that which is causing us so many difficulties.

The changes, in most of the occasions, arise for the necessity that one feels before the problems that the life is posing to him. If these are very numerous, one begins to experience that one needs to order some things and regulate or channel some habits that are not the most appropriate to achieve the goals that one proposes.

At this point we realize that we have nurtured, over time, a series of actions that have not contributed anything to our personal development, so it is time to change direction.

We can only perceive this if we are sufficiently observant and attentive to all this that occurs and that in many cases we are unaware of. We simply let ourselves be guided by a series of mechanisms that in the end

end up dominating us without us being very aware of it.

BE AWARE

This is how we function inside. If we want to generate changes, we must first become aware of what is happening; this is the first starting point.

From there, we can establish changes, substituting some thoughts for others or putting aside those that are useless or toxic, or that have negative consequences.

This can only be achieved if we are aware that these processes occur within, in our own mind.

Once we pay attention to them, we can somehow intervene on them, so that we are not affected by certain mental contents, since we must not deny that every thought is accompanied by an emotion.

Therefore, if we are able to intervene on our own thoughts, we will be able to remove those that cause us some kind of discomfort, or that can influence our emotional state, our psychological well-being.

All that which dwells in our mind can dominate us at any given moment. However, we can free ourselves if we are aware of all this that agitates us in our consciousness. If we realize that all these contents can submerge us in suffering, in which we can lose ourselves for long periods of time.

We cannot allow our mind to take over our inner world, for we will live in a deep sleep far from reality itself. We can get lost in all that tumult of thoughts that move through the length and breadth of our consciousness. Or, we can become paralyzed if we are

dealing with thoughts that cause us to fall into despondency and anguish.

KNOWLEDGE OF OURSELVES

Inside us we have an intelligent system, barely per-
ceptible, that works mechanically without us being
very conscious of it.

Sometimes it can cause us torment, when this system is dominated by a set of negative thoughts that
end up impressing us. These contents take over our
reason and remain there, in our mind, for long periods
of time.

In this way, they mark the direction we have to follow, while, on our part, we do not put any kind of
limitation. We do not pay attention to what is trying to
direct us. We give ourselves to this mechanism, which
is like a mechanical machine, without caring about the
consequences that this can bring us.

It can lead us to confusion, projecting onto our
consciousness a series of elements that are apparently
not comprehensible. Moreover, these contents can
arise in a disordered, impulsive way, so that it is difficult for us to control them.

If we really want to establish changes in our own
inner world - where all these processes that remain for
so long are located - we must be interested in self-
knowledge. This will bring us closer to understanding
all that hidden activity that no one sees, but which
governs us without our having any control over it.

STOP TO OBSERVE

If we stop to observe this calmly, we will realize how this mechanism works; how are the processes behind all this mental activity in which many times we are involved without having control over it. This is the only way to remedy it, to make changes in our way of thinking, in our mental structure.

If we manage to go beyond and take that step, we will achieve enormous results in terms of our way of seeing reality, of interpreting it and of being in the world. Our attitude will change when we face the different difficulties that we face on a daily basis.

Realizing that we function in this way will bring a great number of benefits for us, in many aspects of life; even in our relationships with others, because we will be able to eliminate many prejudices, many beliefs, that we have about those around us, which evidently influence the quality of the relationships we have with them.

LEARNING TO INTERVENE

We have to learn to cultivate in our own mind those contents that are beneficial and positive. This will contribute to a much healthier life, especially on a mental level. We will not be constantly exposed to a halo of confusion derived from all those toxic thoughts that often assail us and that we do not know how to moderate.

If too much negative information accumulates in our mind, it will be harmful. In the end it will blind us and will continue to grow and separate us from who we really are. Everything that spreads through our consciousness without any control on our part will not be good. In these cases we need to move all those elements to another place. We must try to replace them with others before they settle and increase without our consent.

We cannot be mere spectators of all that happens in our mind. We must learn to intervene, in some way, to prevent certain contents from spreading through our consciousness. To do so, we must pay attention to all those representations that are repeated over and over again in our inner voice. We will immediately become aware of those elements that try to create a conflict for us, of the contents that try to cause us some difficulty.

It depends on our own will that we put this into practice. It is not so difficult if we are a little observant of all that happens inside. We will learn to distinguish where is the deception that sometimes our own mind tries to exercise. It will help us to discover the truth, which is hidden behind each and every one of the thoughts that occupy our consciousness.

SEEKING TRANQUILITY

We tend, somehow, to act in a mechanical way, letting our internal system do all the work. We just let ourselves be carried away by all that set of contents that manifest themselves repeatedly.

We must prevent, by all means, that our mind takes over us and forces us to act like a robot, in a mechanical way, without being able to establish any kind of moderation on our part. We have to be aware that we can intervene in this mechanism, that we can reach a certain control over our own thinking.

If we are patient and seek the tranquility to make the appropriate changes, we will manage to modify many internal processes that are at the base of many of our habits that we repeat daily and that are not favorable to us; it is the only way to stop them.

To approach this knowledge of all that happens inside us, it is necessary that we seek that tranquility: those moments where serenity must reign, an inner calm that turns off the momentum of all those unconscious thoughts that trap us constantly.

Once we reach that point, without forcing anything, we can reach moderation. This will allow us to put in order all those reproductions that crowd our consciousness and to which sometimes we cannot find a reasonable explanation.

It will help us to order a little bit all that tumult of elements that many times pile up in our conscience and that cause us an internal obfuscation because they are so numerous that we do not understand much of the information that is there.

19. Search for solutions

I always try to free myself from conflicts, although I do not always succeed. Sometimes they flood practically the totality of my thoughts; then I feel the suffering in me, when they penetrate into the depths of my inner world.

Faced with such confusion, I try to look for solutions to restore tranquility to my state of mind. I place my trust in my experience, in all that I have learned over the years. At such moments I hope that the knowledge I have acquired previously will help me. In such a situation I am aware that I have to change course, that I must not allow myself to be dominated by all that sequence of toxic thoughts that try to organize themselves in my consciousness.

I try to look for a meaning to everything I am thinking, to try to give another sense to my own reasoning.

It is a complex task: it is a matter of ordering the mind a little, observing those contents that are repeated the most, seeing what is strengthening them, what is behind all those ideas that at that moment are running through my mind without any foundation.

I try not to let myself be impressed by all those impulses that are trying to exalt themselves from the depths of my unconscious. I try to interrupt in this way their influence, because otherwise they silently take over me, shaping me, creating a mental structure that in the end becomes a programming that is leading me, that is arranging my actions until it ends up taking control of my own will.

WE SEE THINGS IN THE SAME WAY

We are always inclined to see things in the same way; it is our natural way of seeing the world.

We assimilate everything we perceive around us and this shapes our knowledge of life. All this information, in reality, are fragments that we keep in an arsenal that is our memory; there rest all these data for when we need them.

When we encounter some difficulty and we need to consider some solution, we look back to all that accumulated information from the past in order to fix that problem. Then we get to aggregate a series of data that we put together until we make a decision to get us out of it.

Sometimes, with time, we manage to discover that the solution we chose was not the right one, since we made a decision at that moment that only increased even more the confusion we already had.

Then we feel a daze that we begin to experience when we are aware that some of the solutions we put into practice are not enough to remove all those difficulties.

This may happen because in our analysis we always see things in the same way, or because our thoughts about what is happening to us belong to the same program, so they are always the same; and that is why we cannot find any satisfactory alternative in our ideas about a matter. If they are irrational, they are likely to remain so over time; they will always be there, in the same place. We can only change them if we are aware that we are always making the same decisions about the same problems, when we realize that the same thoughts about that particular issue are always hovering over us.

RECOGNIZING WHAT WE THINK

We have the capacity to transcend all this, to analyze things in a different way, in a calmer way, from serenity.

Then we will be aware of our mistakes, of the position we take in the face of many difficulties. We will realize that many of the operations that we carry out to get out of difficulties are not the most appropriate.

All this allows us, gives us the faculty to conduct our life in a more effective way. If we know how to perceive all these representations that are created in our mind, through thought, we can be aware of them as they present themselves in our consciousness.

Many of these are part of our inner voice, of that inner talk we have with ourselves in which we establish an inner communication through a series of thoughts, sometimes equivocal, that we verbalize in a hidden speech that we only know exists when we stop to observe what is going on in our head.

If we are aware of this talk, we can recognize what we think about a certain matter, so that we can moderate it, reduce what we believe to be wrong, reduce the deception, establish an order, find the truth that is hidden behind all those illusory thoughts that often separate us from the reality of life itself and those around us.

FEELING THE NEED

We allow ourselves to be seduced by the mind, even if what it proposes to us is unreal. We allow ourselves to be enraptured by all those inventions that arise in our consciousness, even if some of them have no logical explanation. We allow ourselves to be confused by all those manifestations that many times make us lose our serenity, that subdue us without previous warning.

In most cases we do not look beyond them. We let them stay there for long periods of time, without caring that they influence our state of mind.

We remain static, doing nothing. We are indifferent to the possible consequences of all those contents that are endlessly illustrated in our mind.

When we lose our serenity we realize that something is happening. Then we are faced with the need to experience some change that will lead us to eliminate all those toxic manifestations that over time have become frequent in our mind.

Most of the time we neglect all this. We are not aware of the importance that all these processes have on our own well-being.

KNOWLEDGE

Continuous exposure to a series of thoughts, which are almost always the same, influences us in every way.

That is why we must learn to stop all this stream of mental contents that become strong in our consciousness by force of constant repetition.

We can only reach inner harmony if we stop, somehow, all these automatic processes that invade us.

We have to look for a way out and face the enormous influence of our own mind. We must learn to manage in a different way all those expressions that move through our consciousness. We cannot allow ourselves to be invaded by all those toxic thoughts that follow one after the other in an uncontrolled way.

We have to learn to somehow cleanse our mind. We cannot just abandon ourselves to its influence, to its activity, because it will end up dominating us.

For all this we need to reach the knowledge of our own mental functioning. If we acquire it, we will know perfectly what alters us, what separates us from what we really are.

It is essential that we reflect on this. It will help us to extinguish everything that is causing us harm.

The knowledge that we can acquire will only come from the observation that we can make about ourselves, from the degree of consciousness that we reach and from the calm that we reach when we seek those moments of silence to explore our inner world.

Then we will reach clarity. Understanding will come, and in those moments we will cease to remain submissive to all those thoughts that are constantly being pushed in our mind without warning.

If we do this practice, we will temper all that noise that often exists inside that only creates inconveniences.

BENEFITS

When we establish changes, we are actually resetting our mind; we are making it possible to produce other thoughts different from the ones that were already there, occupying all the mental space, repeating themselves over and over again in a mechanical way.

We cannot limit ourselves to obey, without further ado, everything that passes through our endless consciousness. We have to overcome that inertia that traps us and that little by little determines us without us realizing it.

It is the best way to put some order in our mind. If we neglect it, it ends up dominating us. In the end, we will live in confusion, subordinated to every thought that arises from our unconscious.

We cannot waste our mental energy in repeating the same contents over and over again. We must put a stop to this process. In this way we will be able to notice that, behind all this structure that is articulated in our mind, there is a space where there is an emptiness that is not occupied by anything.

If we establish changes, we will have a greater facility to leave aside all those representations that occupy our consciousness, that extend throughout our mind and that end up appearing in that inner voice that we all have, in that internal chatter where every thought that appears in our consciousness slips.

It is the best way to disarm, also, many mental programming that we create by force of always repeating the same habits. When we pacify the mind in this way, we will be able to isolate everything negative in us, and that which is causing us emotional damage.

If we eliminate all that mental noise that invades us constantly, an inner peace will spread inside us that will teach us to find calm: that calmness that takes us away from any affliction, from suffering and from everything that causes us anguish, restlessness…

If we want to be free of suffering, the best way is to try to clear our mind. It is the best method to expel everything that does not benefit us; it is the best way to build a new mental structure, much closer to what we really are, in the depths of ourselves.

20. Reflection

Everything that I think will mark my path. In reality, I depend, most of the time, on what goes through my head. It is true that I can end up doing something else, but in these cases I need to stop and observe what I am thinking in order to make the best possible decision.

Let's say that in those moments I become aware of what I have in my conscience. Most of the time I am guided by my own experience when making a decision. In these cases, what I may be thinking at that moment does not have much influence.

Sometimes I am clear about what I should do and I do not let myself be influenced by any other thoughts that may arise in those moments that go in the opposite direction.

On the other hand, at other times, when I have doubts or I do not see clearly what is the best decision, I tend to let myself be carried away by the first thing I have in my head at that moment. This way of acting has probably led me to make many mistakes through-out my life. It may be that on some occasions I have been right without knowing it; I may have taken a direction without knowing beforehand that it was the best option.

In any case, it is always advisable to reflect beforehand and see the consequences of acting in a certain way. There are many thoughts that you cannot trust. They arise suddenly and trap you in such a way that in the end they make you see a reality that is very different from the one that really exists.

We need to be especially careful when making our own interpretations of the world and everything that happens to us. In many cases, our analysis may not be in line with the truth of what is really happening.

THE HABITUAL

It is important to reflect, especially when we have to make important decisions, when we have to choose between several options.

It is advisable not to do it in an automatic and mechanical way, but it is good to make an interval, to be aware in those moments of what we are going to do, of the direction we are going to take.

This can only be achieved if we know how to control ourselves; if we know how to observe ourselves and analyze, even if only briefly, that inner voice that tries to transmit to us the thoughts that at that moment exist in our mind, even if it does it in a repetitive way. If we observe it, we will realize what we are thinking at that moment and the influence that what we are thinking has on our actions and our decisions.

This would be a conscious way of acting, of being in the world; but it is not usual. The normal thing is to have an unconscious attitude, to let ourselves be carried away by our own mind and let it take the reins at all times of what we think, of what we do. We allow without further ado that it is marking us the direction we should follow.

Only when we obtain concrete results, we realize the consequences of our actions. Then we stop, we stop to reflect on the decisions we made at the time and that have had as a consequence the results we are seeing at that moment. We do this when they are negative consequences for us.

If things are going fairly well for us, we don't worry too much about the causes behind them. We usually do it when the results are negative or when things have not turned out as we expected.

Then we try to go back to the beginning, to the original ideas, where the thoughts arose that later were transformed into actions that led us to those concrete results in those cases, to those bad results.

This is our usual way of acting; and it is all because we are used to behaving in an unconscious way. We do not stop, not even for a moment, to evaluate ourselves; to analyze what we are thinking; or to observe that inner voice that repeats itself over and over again, which is composed of all those thoughts that at every moment are circulating in our mind throughout our consciousness.

BENEFITS

Thanks to reflection I can make better decisions; act in a more consistent way; find myself in a certain way with myself.

My reasoning is more consistent, as if there is a better coordination between my ideas; and it also helps me to discover some things about myself that are usually hidden.

It helps me to become aware of my own judgments, of all those thoughts that linger the longest in my own mind, that persevere the most.

I can realize how I fabricate my own beliefs; how my reasonings are initiated.

Thanks to this observation, which I can make of myself, I can realize how my mind is configured, how it creates obstacles that lead to confusion and how I can re-establish serenity.

If I detach myself from all that agitation that envelops me with impetus, through contents that are repeated over and over again in my consciousness, I can escape from the false reality created by my own mind. I can come to understand the world better; I can have a vision more adapted to the truth and take into consideration all those things that are usually hidden behind everything that happens.

Thanks to reflection we can understand how this process works, in such a way that we will be able to make important changes in our way of associating information, of joining thoughts, of using our own reasoning with more sensible judgments closer to the truth.

Through reflection we can become aware of the direction we are heading. We can stop along the way and observe what we are doing. In this way we will be able to evaluate in detail if the path we are following is the right one; or if, on the other hand, it is necessary to make a detour because we are going in the wrong direction. There is always time to rectify.

Only through reflection can we come to understand this mechanism that can muzzle us if we pay too much attention to it.

If we reflect a little, we will realize all that accumulates in our consciousness, which are nothing more than elements that often arise unconsciously and that occupy a space that is becoming larger and larger, until they manage to capture our attention and settle there, for long periods of time.

We will realize that many of these thoughts arise impulsively, taking over our will, without any previous reflection on our part. For this reason, in many occasions, we have irrational ideas that get in the way, that hinder us, that cloud our reason and make us appreciate reality in a wrong way.

This is why it is important that we are aware of them. In this way we will not let ourselves be trapped so easily, because we will always leave a space for a little reflection on these thoughts. In this way, we will immediately detect those thoughts that are negative for us, those that are not beneficial to our own well-being.

Concentrate on what is beneficial

That is why we must concentrate on what we really understand to be beneficial. If we make a mistake, we can then make up for it. Life is an accumulation of experiences from which we learn, which help us to rebuild what we have previously destroyed by our own mistakes, or by a lack of previous knowledge.

We will always have the opportunity to repair what we have damaged without realizing it; to change all those old habits that have been predetermining us without being very conscious of it.

All this is possible if we manage to distinguish the

causes that are behind all our conflicts. Some may be external; but others, on the other hand, may be devised in the deepest part of ourselves, in such a way that they create an internal division that in the end separates us from what we really are, making us see reality in an irrational way, while we remain there, complacent, in the distance, without thinking about the consequences that all this entails.

We cannot remain submissive to all this influence that tries to determine us. If there is no moderation on our part, all these influences will cover us, seducing us, in such a way that in the end they will take away our own will, so that we will not end up being what we really are.

IF WE DO NOT REFLECT

If we do not reflect, we will live determined by the vision of the world imposed on us from outside.

If we do not apply our own criteria and we are not meticulous when analyzing the information that comes to us from the environment in which we live, we get used to follow the guidelines that others set for us, that which society dictates to us at any given moment.

We will not deviate from what is determined from outside; we will allow ourselves to be deceived by all those stimuli that are constantly overwhelming us and that are influencing our decisions and delimiting the direction we should take at any given moment.

If we do not look at ourselves, we will let ourselves be influenced by everything around us. We will let ourselves be dominated by all those close influences that exist in our environment. We will become accustomed to following what others dictate to us; we will do so without any opposition, without first analyzing the consequences of following a certain path.

If we allow ourselves to be guided by everything that is imposed from outside, we will be mistaken, since in the end we will be separated from what we really are; we will move away from our true purpose.

21. Self-knowledge

Our inner richness is extraordinary. We cannot despise it by turning away from what really matters, which is the knowledge that we can have of ourselves, which gives us the ability to become aware of everything that propagates in our mind; to detach ourselves from all those thoughts that cause us harm or discomfort.

We need to come to the knowledge of that wisdom that is hidden in the deepest part of ourselves, that has to do with what we are, beyond the thoughts, beyond our ideas, beyond all those beliefs that we form about life and the world around us.

We must separate ourselves from all this; start to listen to ourselves a little more, to observe that inner voice where all those thoughts that try to dominate us are synthesized, that associate with each other with the aim of showing us the direction to follow.

OBSERVING OUR INNER VOICE

If we want to get to know ourselves, the first thing we must do is to pay attention to this voice that speaks to us: to that inner speech that we all have and that is marking the way, that somehow is influencing us in everything we do, in what we think or in the decisions we have to take to go solving the difficulties that are presented to us.

We will only find ourselves if we are able to decipher all those messages that are hidden in our inner voice, where the different thoughts that arise in our mind are manifested. We will know ourselves much better if we observe ourselves, if we pay attention to all that is manifested in our inner world, which is embodied in our consciousness and that tries to guide us, to lead us, to determine us.

Self-knowledge begins when we start to look inwards, towards our inner world. If we move away from the material world, from that world that is out there and that tries to influence us through all those stimuli that it presents to us, in the context in which we live.

Therefore, observing that inner voice that we all carry inside, will help us to know ourselves better, to understand why we focus our attention on certain issues or why we act in a particular way.

It is just a matter of paying attention to our own inner voice, because that is where everything that is in our consciousness at any given moment is summarized, which is where the most important thoughts that we have throughout the day and to which we give greater importance are manifested. Those are the ones that are repeated the most, and that is why they appear unceasingly in that inner voice that is like an internal dialogue we have with ourselves, which seems to never end.

If we pay attention to all this, we will know ourselves much better; and this will help us to establish changes within our internal world, in our own personality, in our way of thinking, in our beliefs and in our own judgments, in the way we relate to others and in the way we are in the world.

We will have a different attitude towards life, towards the problems and difficulties we face at any given moment. We will have many more tools, with all those that are hidden there, inside, beyond our own mind, our thoughts, which are often misleading, since they are not adapted to the truth, because sometimes they are nothing more than invented images that have nothing to do with the world in which we live, because they are only the fruit of our own imagination.

PERSONAL HISTORY

With time we become aware of the consequences of having acted in a mechanical and repetitive way, we are not conscious at that moment; but later, when we observe the results obtained from our actions, that is when we become aware of our way of acting and the causes that have led us to behave in that way; of the ideas behind our behaviors and attitudes. But this only happens if we observe ourselves, if we become aware of what is going on in our inner world.

All this leads us to the knowledge of what we are, of the causes that have led us to be what we are. We will become aware of the influence that all the experiences of the past have had on us: the events that have happened around us and that in some way have influenced our way of acting. We will be aware of the interpretations we have made, of all those experiences we have had the chance to undergo.

All this is transformed into information that we accumulate in our memory, that we have stored there, for when we need it.

There, in a way, is our personal history: the experiences we have lived through and the difficulties we have had to go through; the problems we have had to overcome... All this becomes an accumulation of knowledge that helps us to survive and move forward.

Much of this information may not be correct, it may be wrong, because it is only the result of a series of subjective and personal interpretations that we made at the time of what happened to us. It is possible that part of that information is incorrect because we were not objective enough at the time, or because we did not reflect enough when those specific experiences took place.

In this sense, many of our reasoning may be wrong, not logical, not in accordance with the truth. They may be conclusions that we reach at a certain moment and that we finally convert into information that we keep in our memory and that remains there, for long periods of time, until we discover that there is other more valuable information regarding that particular subject and that may be more in line with the truth.

But all this is given to us by our own experience, by learning, by the knowledge we acquire throughout our lives.

Our natural way of acting is to let ourselves be carried away by what our mind is proposing at every moment; although we always try to look for a sense: to do things under a certain direction, to lead us towards a concrete place, with a certain end. But throughout this process, we let ourselves be guided by our mind, by the thoughts that arise automatically. We abandon ourselves to this mechanism and allow it to direct us, to lead us.

BENEFITS

When we connect with ourselves everything stops; it is as if everything is ordered, put in its place. We are scattered, without knowing who we are, without knowing the meaning of the things we do. It is necessary to find ourselves in order to find out. It is the only way to organize our inner world.

If we come to a knowledge of ourselves, we will understand the processes that take place within our own mind; we will know how to decipher the mysteries that are hidden behind this mechanism that we all carry inside, this inner voice that works constantly, that shows us one thought after another, while we follow the guidelines of everything that it is proposing to us at every moment.

When one finds oneself, everything is seen in a different way. In normal conditions we see everything in a superficial way, we do not stop in the details, in the details, in all those aspects that are behind the appearances and that is what really matters.

When one knows oneself, one knows how to look inside oneself and learns to discard what is not useful, to set aside what is not important for its true purpose. He knows how to distinguish clearly where the truth of things is, from what he sees, both outside and inside himself.

We can discover all this if we look inward and pay attention to what that inner voice, which we all have, tries to transmit to us.

22. Transformation

Transformation begins when all those thoughts that separate us from ourselves begin to fade. When we banish from our mind everything that makes us experience suffering, a change begins to develop within us that transports us to wellbeing.

If we contemplate all that happens inside us, we will be able to reach the true transformation, because we will have the opportunity to observe everything that causes us that division that affects our peace and in this way we will be able to moderate it.

We will become aware of what activates our own suffering, of how those negative and uncomfortable thoughts are born and how a mental structure that influences our way of seeing the world, our way of interpreting reality, is put together.

We must begin to take care of ourselves, and the best way to do this is by extending our gaze to everything that is being represented in our mind at any given moment.

If the contents are not appropriate and we allow them to accompany us permanently and we do not ignore them, we will end up living in a continuous unhappiness because of the attachment to this kind of thoughts, which in most cases are painful.

PUTTING EVERYTHING IN ITS PLACE

It is clear to me that all of life's experiences have an effect on me. They can submerge me in anguish, when they are negative; or they are the beginning of something new, the beginning of a small personal transformation that somehow serves me to leave behind many setbacks in the form of obstacles that from time to time settle in my mind and confuse me. So I have no choice but to put everything back in its place to try to continue on the right path.

I try to do this when frustration takes hold of me, for example. In those moments I try to look for an explanation, reconsidering what I am thinking.

This strategy is useful to me, because in this way, besides establishing a communication with myself, I try to stop what is instigating me inside, which is usually some idea, or some irrational belief that has been triggered without me being very aware of it.

INTERNAL DIALOGUE

Another thing I do is to pay attention to my internal dialogue, to that talk that I often have with myself when I am not in the company of other people. When I look closely at what I am saying to myself, I can explore, in a clear way, the kind of thoughts I am using, the kind of ideas I am planting in my mind and why I am choosing those and not others that are somewhat more constructive and beneficial to me.

Subsequently I become aware, thanks to this observation, of the need to change course: the inclination of all those contents that take over my consciousness and that little by little are introducing me into a toxic reality that I cannot eliminate until I contemplate it with the calm that is required.

Observe

If you examine yourself and know how to penetrate into your inner world and see the magnitude of what exists there, you will become aware of your inner chatter, of all those explanations that you give yourself about those things that happen to you. You will realize that this is where the confusion begins, in those statements that you make about the events that happen to you.

Your internal chatter is the output of your own thoughts, which are chained together until they engrave in you a way of seeing reality that is then embodied in that inner voice that does not disappear, which is constantly repeated through comments that you say to yourself and that often are not rational or reflective, as they arise unconsciously through a series of expressions that occupy your consciousness.

The best strategy is to observe all this through silence. Then you will be able to transform yourself, to know how all these processes that seem indestructible work. It is the only way to make them disappear so that they do not progress, so that they do not grow inside you and transform you into a robot that acts in a mechanical way.

If you are capable of observing all this, you will return to sanity, to your own freedom; you will move away from the noise of your own mind, isolating all those contents that are repeated over and over again and that are influencing your way of interpreting the world.

DO NOT LET YOURSELF BE CAPTIVATED

Never let yourself be captivated by what arises in your mind, nor let yourself be surprised by all those elements that constantly appear in your consciousness that are born from the depths of your unconscious. They are only diffuse contents, components that try to unite with each other to form a structure of thoughts that in many occasions are closer to fiction than to reality itself.

If you allow yourself to be overcome by them, they will begin to agitate you inside, to erase your tranquility, and will end up dominating you, simulating a false reality that will absorb you. So you will live in an illusory world, invented, far from reality.

If you persevere in following that voice that repeats itself within you and let yourself be carried away by its outbursts, you will be feeding your own destruction, strengthening the confusion within you.

INTERRUPTING THE MECHANISM

I have learned to be aware that in order to obtain results it is necessary to go beyond, to get to clear my head of all those things that can plunge me into a darkness totally far from reason.

This also helps me, at specific moments, not to let myself be dominated by all those toxic thoughts that register in my mind in a hasty way. I always try to replace them with others that make me regain control of myself, that link me with what I really am and make me come out of the darkness.

I understand that the only way to recover the best of myself is to free myself from the bonds of thought, especially when it remains suspended in the past, trying to resurrect what was negative.

For this it is good to get used to break with all those vicious circles that often plunge us into disaster. Many times they are kept there by ignorance, by habit, or by a certain disinterest on our part.

It is always advisable to try to find solutions, to interrupt in some way this insensitive mechanism that limits us, that takes over our own judgments and that leads us to the abyss on many occasions.

ABOUT THE AUTHOR

Manuel Triguero has a degree in Psychology from the Pontifical University of Salamanca (Spain).

He is the author of books related to self-help and personal development. As a counselor, he has had the opportunity to assist a large number of people on an individual basis.

Many of the reflections that appear in his books are born from experience and his own observation. They are tips that he tries to share as a means of support for those who are going through difficulties.

His idea is also to provide content and tools to all those interested in personal growth and self-improvement, thus contributing to the improvement of the world we live in.

Printed in Great Britain
by Amazon